Kendal Green

A GEORGIAN WASTELAND RECLAIMED

by
John & Jean Coopey

✱

John Coopey   *Jean Coopey*

HELM
PRESS

With acknowledgement to the assistance
of the Curwen Archive Trust

Published by Helm Press
10 Abbey Gardens, Natland, Kendal, Cumbria LA9 7SP
Tel: 015395 61321
E-MAIL: HelmPress@natland.freeserve.co.uk

Copyright – John & Jean Coopey 2002

First published 2002

Typeset in Minion

ISBN 0 9540497 3 X

Typeset and printed by Miller Turner Printers, The Sidings, Beezon
Fields, Kendal, Cumbria LA9 6BL

Front cover: Photograph taken by Stengal of Kendal Green in the early 1900s
Back cover: Aerial view of Kendal Green taken in the 1970s by Peter Thornton

CONTENTS

Aerial photograph of Kendal Green taken in the 1970s

INTRODUCTION

URING OUR FIRST year living on Kendal Green we searched for books on the history of the town and especially the area in which we had settled. Soon we came across Roger Bingham's *Social History of Kendal* but, despite its 448 pages covering the period from the Neolithic era to 1993, Kendal Green is mentioned only twice and one of those references is to a public house of that name in Windermere Road. However some material was gleaned from Bingham and other sources about, for example, the Green's history as part of 'Low Tenter Fell' when it was bedecked with cloth hung out to stretch on tenters and about the Quakers who were influential in its development as a residential area.

Even so, we thought there must be something else worth discovering and attempting to record about its more recent history particularly the period since the building of the first houses on the Green in the Victorian era. So, after about two years living here, we began to think seriously about writing some sort of history for people who live on the Green and others in Kendal who might also be interested. Near neighbours encouraged us in the venture as did the twenty or so people who attended the inaugural meeting of an informal association of Kendal Green residents held in May 2000.

They, and many others who live on the Green, together with friends and acquaintances in Kendal and those who responded to our letters in the Westmorland Gazette, have provided invaluable information by researching the deeds of their houses, loaning us their deeds and photographs or drawing on their memories and other records about life on the Green. Without their help this account of Kendal Green's history could not have been written, so we are delighted to dedicate it to them:

Mary Bagenal, Christian Barnes, Kevin & Debbie Bell, Tim & Toni

Bennett, Michael Bottomley of Haigh Architects, Jen Bowyer, Peter & Christine Briggs, Robert & Christine Burgess, Roger & Jane Burrow, Diane Burton, Dorothy Byass, Marjorie Crossley, Michael Crossley, Rob David, Richard & Angela Day, Gerald & Andrea Dean, Joan Deighton, Harry Dixon, Pat Dixon, Elaine Dunnington, Robert & Jilly Edwards, Norman & Ann Ellis, Freda Exley, John Floyd, Peter & Sheila Fox, Phil Gordon & Kay Taylor, Eric & Joan Green, Martin & Helen Greenbank, Geoffrey Hodkinson, Edward & Di Holt, Colin Martindale, Mike & Joan Mellor, Chris & Anne Michalak, Richard Pealing & Hilary Webb, Elizabeth Pursell, Alan & Rosemary Reed, Jim Richardson, Peter Rigg, Colin & Sue Rowley, David and Eileen Russell, Ian Shaw, Jean Simpson, Jeffrey Stokes, George & Margaret Taylor, Nancy Walker, Alan Waters, Derek Watson, Barbara Webb, Dale & Anne Williams, Jack Williams, Will & Sheila Williams, Danny & Sally Willis, Tessa Wilson and Marion Winchester.

The architectural commentary on Kendal Green houses was provided by Richard Day. We appreciate greatly both his insights and his willingness to endure with us a slow circuit of the Green one bitterly cold Sunday afternoon in February. We made notes of his observations as the three of us stood shivering before each house in turn.

Although not a resident of the Green, Jean Simpson has taken a particularly close interest in our project. In effect she has acted – unprompted and with great persistence – as a volunteer researcher, drawing especially on her knowledge of the Society of Friends. We thank her for her unstinting support and friendship and for enriching our appreciation of the work of her Quaker grandfather, Arthur Simpson, wood carver and furniture designer, who plays a part in the narrative which follows.

We are also greatly indebted to the curators of the Cumbria Record Office in Kendal – especially Mr Richard Hall and Mrs Kathy Strickland – and the curator of the local history section of Kendal Library, Mrs Jackie Fay. Despite our 'greenness' in researching original documents – even having the temerity to bring pens into the County Hall reading room – they seemed to delight with us when something particularly interesting turned up.

The advice and encouragement given to us by local historians – John Marsh, Arthur Nicholls and John Satchell – is much valued. We also thank John Satchell for providing insights into the lives of residents of the Green during the Edwardian era contained in his book *Family Album,* and for his permission to use photographs from that and other books he has written.

As to the many other photographs and illustrations in the book we offer many thanks to the Brewery Arts Centre, Cumbria Records Office,

Kendal Library, Museum of Lakeland Life at Abbot Hall, the Windermere Nautical Trust, Michael Crossley, Pat Dixon, Rose Steele, Barbara Webb and Tessa Wilson. We are especially indebted to Geoffrey Thompson for the variety of material he so willingly provided and to Percy Duff for the very free access he gave to images from the Margaret Duff Collection of photographs of Kendal. Without this wide set of contributions our narrative would be a much duller read.

As far as possible we have given those who provided information an opportunity to confirm that our interpretation is consistent with the spirit and content of the original material. That said, we take full responsibility for any errors of fact or interpretation that remain.

Finally, we gratefully acknowledge the assistance of the Curwen Archives Trust in providing a generous grant towards the costs of publishing this book.

Information on sources used is provided at the end of the text, both in general terms and in references to specific items. The latter are listed by chapter in order of the numbers placed throughout the narrative. The story that we have shaped from these diverse sources is what might be called a 'micro–history' in the sense that, even though a broad context is provided, it deals primarily with a very small place over a very short period of time in the span of English history as a whole. The piece of land on which Kendal Green is sited extends over less than 22 acres and has been part of Kendal for only 235 years, one of the lower stretches of fell land given to the town by George III in 1767. As for its name, 'Kendal Green', this was decided 138 years ago when the first houses were being built there.

John Coopey Jean Coopey

John & Jean Coopey
November 2002

THE GREEN IN ITS EARLY CONTEXT

I N THIS FIRST chapter Kendal Green is placed in its wider context in three senses. First we examine its origins as part of the Kendal Fell lands that were granted to the town by the King in the 18th century; then we refer to what had already been built in the local area prior to and during the early period of building on the Green; finally, we consider the availability of funding from the 1860s provided by banks and building societies.

ORIGINS

The place now called Kendal Green was earlier part of lands that belonged to the Crown. When Kendal petitioned the King in about the year 1683 that these lands be granted to the town they were described as 'a parcel of waste ground called Dob Freer, which is all the common pasture that belongs to the town, and is no more than a hill full of rocks and stones'. However, It was not until the seventh year of George III's reign, in 1767, that the plea was granted, when an Act of Parliament allowed for enclosing part of Kendal Fell to be administered by the Kendal Fell Trust, covering an area of about 158 acres.

The Trustees consisted of 'the mayor for the time being and twelve inhabitants of the burgh... owners of property of the yearly value of £10, and rated and assessed to that amount'. They were empowered to let out land to rent and to use any income derived in this and other ways from the Fell lands 'for the use of the poor there, and for cleansing and enlightening the streets of the borough'. However the High and Low Tenter Fells were not to be ploughed up but left for use in woollen manufacture while

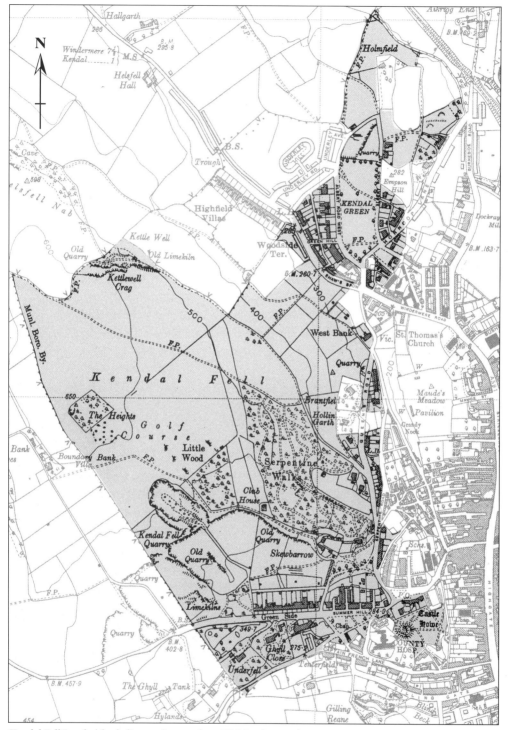

Kendal Fell Lands (shaded) superimposed on OS Map (c. 1938)

Bowling Fell was to be left open for the inhabitants of the town 'to walk upon'.

Trustees were drawn from local wealthy and influential townspeople especially those in business or trade; for example, at least three of the original members appointed in 1767 were hosiers. Dissenters too – who, being excluded from key institutions such as the corporation and established church, tended to make their way in business – played a prominent part, providing at least three of the first group of Trustees: Samuel Gawthrop and two Quakers, John Wakefield I and George Braithwaite.[1]

Quakers built up extensive trading networks both within the Kendal area and more widely across the north of England based in part on relationships with Friends elsewhere, on their considerable geographic mobility, a tendency for intermarriage among Quaker families and the entrepreneurial skills of those such as John Wakefield I, 1738 to 1811. Apprenticed to a shearman dyer he branched out in 1764 to build a gunpowder mill at Sedgwick to manufacture black blasting powder, the first in the country not sited near the Thames estuary. He also started one of the first banks in Kendal and built a brewery there. The skills and enterprise that he and other Quakers showed, and the business networks within which they flourished, were put to the service of the Fell Trust over a period of 140 years following the implementation of the 1767 Act.

In carrying out its dual role of administering 158 acres of the fellside and providing finance for the town the Trust became in effect 'an agency of local government' in parallel with the town's existing corporation. As such it played an important part in the development of the town well into the 19th century although Marshall[2] claims that the Trust was not ideally suited for these duties and, hence, did not perform them well. Certainly it seems strange with hindsight that its role had not been assigned, from the beginning, to the borough corporation.

The extent of Kendal Fell as drawn on a map of 1847 by John Watson Jun.[3] is represented by the shaded portion of an extract from a much more recent Ordnance Survey (OS) map on page 12. Its boundary makes several detours to exclude land already privately owned and a detour in the south–east to include Bowling Fell on which Castle Howe stands.

That part of the fell that now includes Kendal Green was known as 'Tenterfell' on maps dated 1787 and 1833, but by 1853 it had become 'Low Tenter Fell' by contrast with 'High Tenterfell' on the higher land above the other end of what is now Queen's Road. The coarse woollen cloth produced in and around Kendal was stretched out on 'tenter frames' arranged in rows in these areas and other parts of Kendal outside the fell lands, such as at Goose Holme on the river near Thorny Hills.

The Act of 1767 allowed that 'the right of shearmen and other manufacturers of Kendal in the tenters shall remain to them whole and entire and they may hereafter use the said tenters, repair the same or erect new ones upon the said High and Low Tenter Fells as their occasion shall require'. Tenter frames were shaped like fences about four feet six inches high built along terraces created on the fell side. The cloth was hung from oak pegs attached at six inch intervals along wooden frames but in the 19th century the hooks and, later, the frames themselves, were made of iron. It is claimed that the frames were liable to stain the cloth and that some of it was so overstretched that it shrank badly when first washed.

Demonstration of how cloth was hung from a tenter frame, photographed in 1967 on High Tenterfell.

On Todd's map of 1788 tenter terraces and frames proliferate on Low Tenter Fell. By 1853, the date of a Hoggarth map, only nine tenter frames are shown, the same number as on the later Ordnance Survey (OS) map on a survey carried out in 1858. None at all are shown on the 1898 OS map by which time the growing use of steam power and new mills built with indoor drying sheds had made the outdoor frames obsolete. The photograph, of Kendal Green from the air, shows clearly the remains of the terraces on which tenter frames had stood at the southern end of the woodland, now obscured by a copse planted more recently.

The effect of these various changes in the use of the Fell was reflected in the Kendal Fell Act of 1861 which repealed most of the provisions of the 1767 Act. It stated that 'if any land set apart for tenter–grounds shall not be used as such by any person entitled to do so, for the space of any five consecutive years, such land may be used by the Trustees for other purposes…'. Presumably it was this change that gave the Trustees the authority in 1867 to sanction the removal of the foundations of two of the Green's tenter rows by the Guardians of the Kendal Union who had responsibility for the management of the Workhouse.

The Trustees' scope to find other purposes for the land was extended considerably by the power the 1861 Act conferred on them to grant leases for the building of houses on Kendal Fell lands and to sell land for the making of roads. However, one clause of the Act contained a proviso that two pieces of land, identified in a separate schedule, should be 'set apart for the use of the inhabitants of Kendal, for recreation ground, and for the purpose of drying clothes...'. The two sites were Bowling Fell – 'containing by admeasurement, two acres three roods and twenty-nine perches' – and 'six acres of land on the north side of, and adjoining to the road leading from the House of Correction Hill to Greenbank, and bounded on the east by gardens belonging to the said township lands, and on the north and west by the said township lands'. This latter clause referred to Kendal Green.

The 1861 Act had its roots in attempts made in 1848 by liberal reformers of Kendal, supported by the Fell Trust, to introduce an amending bill principally to free up building land and, hence, to provide the town 'with the financial means of expansion'. This was how they sought to overcome the limits on development imposed by the 1767 Act's prohibition of building on the Fell. Economic growth was being constrained and the town's work force obliged to seek accommodation in already overcrowded houses. As a result land prices were rising rapidly and housing standards falling 'even further than before in the static land market'.

Despite this seemingly strong case certain proposals in the draft bill, to improve sewers and streets and to impose better control of the construction and repair of public and private property, threatened vested interests in the town. So, 'after much politicking, accompanied by allegations of packed meetings, the reformers were defeated'.[4]

After another defeat of a much watered-down bill the issue of building land lay dormant until 1860 when the Kendal Fell Trust was asked at a public meeting to press for the freeing up of the lands they administered 'for building and other purposes thereby supplying the growing demand for additional houses and at the same time largely increasing the revenues to be derived by the ratepayers of Kendal...'. The issue was taken up by a Trustee, John Whitwell, with his colleagues on the Trust; a sub-committee then drafted proposals that eventually led to the passage on 17th May 1861 of the Kendal Fell Amendment Act. This released land for the purpose of recreation and public building.[5]

It seems, however, as we shall see in the case of the development of Kendal Green, that the use of the new freedom to build did not give priority to the building of workers' cottages. The first sale of Fell land specifically for this purpose was not until 1866 when Whitwell bid for plots to be used in this way. Two years later a large number of sites put up for auction were withdrawn on failing to reach the expected price. While some of the better paid workers were able to benefit, most were left to live in unfit houses.

The conditions in which the poorest of them lived was starkly revealed by an outbreak of typhoid in 1873 and 1874. In the latter year Matthew DeRome, an Estate Agent and strong supporter of the town's building societies who later became a Kendal Fell Trustee, was 'summonsed for owning unfit houses…'. In 1875 a survey carried out by the council revealed many more unhealthy houses which encouraged Kendal newspapers to press for 'as great and as urgent an improvement in the conditions of its workers' dwellings as the large towns'.[6]

Meanwhile the Fell Trustees were busy fulfilling their duties under the new 1861 Act guided by a set of 'Bye-Laws' which they had passed and approved in September 1863. These covered the means of securing the regular attendance of Trustees at meetings through a system of fines for unsanctioned absence, the regulation of the use of the quarries, limekilns, other Fell lands and 'places set apart for public recreation', which included Low Tenter Fell. The bye-laws gave the Trust the power to regulate the use of Serpentine Walks and to fine 'any Person placing any erections upon or breaking down or injuring any trees, seats, erections, buildings or fences on, or removing any soil, samel[†], or gravel from, any part of the said lands belonging to the said Trustees without the leave of the said Trustees…'.[7]

THE BUILT ENVIRONMENT

By 1861 when the Kendal Fell Amendment Act came into force a significant amount of development had already taken place in the surrounding area. This included a number of key buildings referred to below, all of which can be seen on the extract from the first OS map of north Kendal opposite.

Green Road factory and farm

The buildings nearest to the Green were the old factory on Green Road immediately opposite the bottom of the Green – now converted to flats – and the houses on the corner of Green Road and Kendal Green opposite the factory. The factory is shown on earlier maps as belonging to J. Gandy

† A hard loamy gravel (*Rollinson: The Cumbrian Dictionary of Dialect, Tradition & Folklore*)

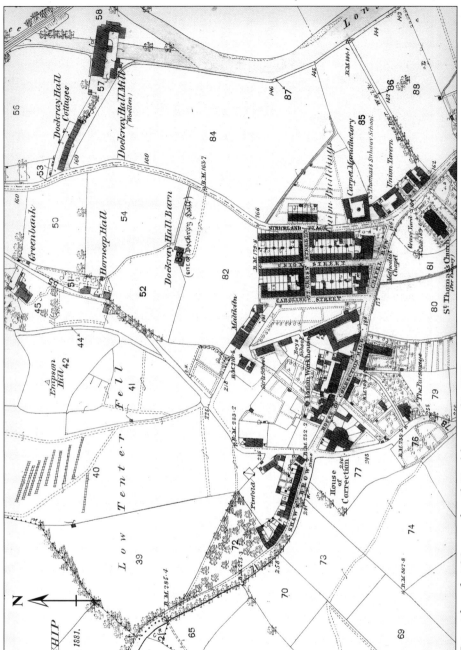

Extract from first OS map of north Kendal surveyed in 1858.

The 'old factory' photographed from the Green

probably referring to James Gandy the woollen manufacturer of Dockwray Hall Mill. There is also evidence that he occupied the tenter frames on Prickley Fell in 1836. So the factory was probably used in the woollen trade.

The small group of dwellings opposite the factory shown on the map still stands, consisting of numbers 10, 14, 16 and 18 Green Road – the latter two virtually on Kendal Green – and the enclosure, now labelled 'yard 12', in which there are two cottages with access between Nos. 10 and 14. In 1861, however, this complex may still have been farm buildings: No. 16 a barn, 18 a farmhouse and the buildings in yard 12 some form of shippon.

Horncop Hall and Greenbank

On the right hand side down Horncop Lane was *Horncop Hall* and just beyond, on the rise of land to the left, *Greenbank*; both houses are still in use. Just up Horncop lane from the latter house was a cock pit the remains of which could still be seen in the 20th century until a bungalow was built on that site.

An early photograph of Horncop Hall taken before the building of bungalows in Ashleigh Road obscured this view.

Kendal to Windermere Railway and Dockwray Hall Mills

About a hundred yards from the bottom of Horncop Lane to the left along Burneside Road a bridge of the Kendal to Windermere Railway already carried the line from the centre of Kendal before it turned towards the next stop at Burneside. The railway had been open 17 years by the time the first houses were built on Kendal Green.

Not far along Burneside Road nearer to the Town was Dockwray Hall Mills, sited on the river just before the grounds in which the Courthouse now stands. In 1809 the mill buildings, said to have originated in the medieval period, were put up for sale, containing four separate mills used for different purposes. The Quaker family firm of Messrs. Gandy and Sons, wool merchants and drysalters, purchased the mills which they proceeded to rebuild in 1816–17 to a design by Francis Webster. After a disastrous fire in 1824 only the walls remained standing but the mills were quickly rebuilt. Six years later the buildings were extended for use as a marble factory and John Atkinson took over part of the mill complex for carpet weaving. Then, when Gandy stopped trading in 1850, John Whitwell's firm took over all of the textile mills for carpet manufacture. In the 1920s, after a period when the mills were empty during the post-war depression, they were used as an artificial silk mill.

Operations ceased entirely during the Great Depression of the early

1930s and the mill buildings were demolished over a period of many years starting in 1940. The chimney stood until the late 1960s and even now some signs remain including at least one building used as a furniture warehouse at the entrance to the industrial estate sited where the mill stood. Along the left-hand side of Dockray[†] Hall Road leading to the estate is a typical terrace of mill workers' cottages.[8]

The Maltkiln

Just down Caroline Street on the left-hand side was a maltkiln in the position it occupied on the first street map of Kendal produced by John Todd in 1787. Older Kendalians know this part of Caroline Street as Maltkiln Hill, often pronounced Mawky Hill.

Malting, the first stage in beer making, allows grains of barley to germinate so that their starch is converted into sugar; the conversion is then stopped by drying the grain in a kiln. The process requires more space than the average 19th century brewery could afford so tended to become a specialised activity. Once dried sufficiently the malt was delivered to local breweries for the fermentation process when other ingredients such as hops and yeast are added.[9] In the earlier period of beer making the brewing was done at the inn or public house itself, as revealed in a reference to one of the six public houses owned by Christopher Robinson the original proprietor of the Caroline Street maltkiln. His Bowling Green Tavern was described as having a 'brew house, stabling and appurtenances situated on Beast Banks'.

The Workhouse

In the same block of land to the south-east of Low Tenter Fell was the Workhouse, straddling the corner made by the bend in Caroline Street. It was built by the Kendal Fell trustees in 1768 as part of their responsibility under the 1767 Act to apply the profits arising from their management of the fell lands 'for and towards the relief, maintenance and employment of the poor of the township of Kendal, and for erecting or purchasing proper buildings and edifices for that purpose, and furnishing such buildings'.

Nearby was 'the vagrant ward', where a house stood in which vagrants were billetted for short periods. To qualify for this they had to apply to the

† At some time in the Mill's life its name changed from Dockwray to Dockray

Facing page: Dockwray Hall Mills from down river showing the tail race which delivered water back to the Kent after it had powered the wheels. Shallow pools, overhung by bushes, are all that remains of the race.

The master's house set within the Workhouse buildings. As here, the surrounding gardens and grounds were cultivated to help feed the residents.

Borough Police Court for a ticket to the 'Vagrant Ward' which entitled them to a supper and bed then breakfast the following morning. In return they were required to labour for two hours, for example, in quarry work.

In 1835 the Workhouse was extended and its administration placed in the hands of the 'Kendal Union' created as part of the national 'Poor Law Union' established under legislation recently enacted. As we have seen already the Kendal Union had an interest in Low Tenter Fell, a theme that will be developed later.

The 'Blue Buildings'

In the period 1820 to 1822 a large block of terrace houses was built east of the Workhouse, including those in the bottom part of Caroline Street but also in Cross Street, Union Street and Strickland Place fronting Burneside Road. The Kendal Union Building Society, the first in Kendal, was the source of mutual funding for these houses. The foundation stone was laid in June 1820 and 84 houses were built by March 1823 at a cost of £8,000 including streets, pumps and water courses.

However, the society's activities became embroiled in electoral contests which took place between 1818 and the early 1820s. Some freeholders of Kendal, already the focus of demands for radical reforms to the process of enfranchisement and selection of parliamentary candidates for Westmorland, supported candidates put forward by the Whigs ('blues'). They were in vigorous and sometimes violent opposition to those proposed by the Tories ('yellows') who depended for their endorsement on the political power of the Lowther family. Short-term tactics were tanta-

The Union Street name plate with date stone

mount to buying votes, whereas longer term the intention was to win over men who were enfranchised by virtue of their being freeholders of land or property worth two pounds. So there was considerable incentive to try to capture the votes of those who bought the new houses.

This tactic was expressed most dramatically in an advertisement that appeared in the *Kendal Chronicle* on 6th February 1819, announcing the sale of '9 freehold houses, each house making a vote, situated on House of Correction Hill... N.B. None need apply but Blues'.[10] Such events caused the whole development to be nick-named 'the Blue Buildings'. It seems, however, that although the Building Society did have clear sympathies for

---

To be Sold by Private Contract,

NINE Freehold DWELLING-HOUSES ; each House making a Vote ; situate on the House of Correction Hill, Kendal. ·

For further Particulars apply to James Martindale, the owner, on the Premises.

N. B. None need apply but *Blues.*

Kendal, Jan. 5, 1819.

---

the more radical Whig position, the advertisement was placed by James Martindale who, though the vendor of the nine houses, was not involved in the management of the Building Society. His intervention preceded by sixteen months the laying of the foundation stone.[11]

Wesleyan Chapel and St. Thomas' Church

Nearby, the Kendal Wesleyan Methodists opened their first purpose-built chapel in 1808 on the lower part of House of Correction Hill, spanning Union Street and Strickland Place. A Sunday School was opened in the building in 1816, one of the first Sunday Schools in the district which, within ten years, had attracted almost 200 children. Given the lack of provision for basic education in the town they were taught how to read and write 'as well as the truths of the bible'.[12] The Sunday School continued in the new Wesleyan Chapel built on the same site in 1882, now Stricklandgate Methodist Church.

St. Thomas' Church was consecrated in 1837 and its parsonage erected on what is now Queen's Road in 1854. A Sunday School had been in exis-

Looking up 'House of Correction Hill' showing the Wesleyan Chapel on the right, Town View beyond on the left and the prison at the top, dominating the surrounding area.

tence since 1833; the first meeting was held on 2nd August of that year 'in the building still called 'The Factory', situated on the Fell above the Workhouse… under the superintendence of John Gandy'.[13] This is almost certainly the building mentioned above now converted to flats on Green Road which, on the 1847 map of Kendal Fell Lands, was shown as belonging to J. Gandy. The school was moved in 1841 to a permanent building on the corner of Stricklandgate and the Burneside road opposite St. Thomas' Church and took on full primary school status in 1847. Next door along Strickland Place was the Kent carpet factory one of the first mills in Kendal devoted to carpet manufacture.

Town View

Up the hill from St. Thomas' Church was Town View, the Georgian terrace of three houses built in 1831 end-on to House of Correction Hill. Nearby, on both sides of the Hill, were blocks of houses sited running up to the junction of Queen's Road and Green Road. There was a public house at No. 11 called *Kendal Green* – owned by Samuel Burdett and still listed in 1906 under Alfred Winder – then, just before Green Road, was a Post

Office. Above the junction, backing on to Low Tenter Fell, stood the terrace of houses on Shaw's Brow, now Windermere Road.

The House of Correction

In the corner between the road up from Stricklandgate and Queen's Road was the local prison, called earlier the 'House of Correction' from which the hill took its name. In the 19th Century its enormous bulk dominated the area but when it was established two centuries earlier under the provisions of Poor Law Acts of 1601 and 1640 it was housed in quite a modest building. Later improvements included a complete rebuilding in 1785–6 and further alterations in 1817 and 1820. Massive walls were constructed at that time using stone from Kettlewell Quarry, on the Heights just below the golf course. It was brought down along a tramway which followed the bridle-way now known as 'The Tram', emerging onto what is now Queen's Road just below the Lakeland Vegetarian Guest House, *Low Slack*. The term 'House of Correction' became obsolete after the Prison Act of 1877 when its official title was changed to 'Her Majesty's Prison, Kendal'.

It is not known how local residents received this news. They tended to favour 'Belle Hill' as their address instead of 'House of Correction Hill', a local difficulty that was resolved for some when the name *Windermere*

Looking down on the Prison from a position overlooking Windermere Road above the junction with Queen's Road

Road was formally adopted although others continued to use the 'assumed' name.

Grandy Nook

Up behind the House of Correction was 'Grandy Nook' which still stands not far along Low Fell Side. It was originally the home of Thomas Sandes who was Mayor in 1647–8 and the founder of Sandes Hospital and the Blue Coat School in Highgate. Grandy Nook's date stone is engraved with the initials of Thomas and Katherine Sandes and the date, 1659.

FINANCIAL INSTITUTIONS

The developments that took place on the Green in the 1860s and 1870s – to create buildings, roads, sewers and other services – would have required considerable financial resources. For example, in today's terms some £2.4 million would be required to finance the building of the sixteen houses of *Wood Lea* and *Beechwood* terraces. Local banks which could have provided finance had existed for almost a century and building societies for over thirty years.

Banks

During the second half of the 18th century the monopoly the Bank of England enjoyed in the printing of bank notes ended and in towns across England 'country' banks were established, so-called to distinguish them from 'The Bank'. In Kendal two banks opened on the same day, 1st January 1788, both involving Quakers. In Stramongate the bank of Maude, Wilson and Crewdson was created through the partnership of an Anglican – Joseph Maude, a successful businessman and 'offcomer' who had lived in the town for only twelve years – and a Quaker, Thomas Crewdson. The other bank was set up in Stricklandgate by John Wakefield I, a leading member of the local Society of Friends and renowned entrepreneur.

On the retirement in 1830 of the last Maude to serve in the former bank, it was renamed W. D. Crewdson & Sons, the Wilsons having withdrawn from the bank during an earlier banking crisis. Then, ten years later, the bank was amalgamated with Wakefield's to form Kendal Bank which moved in 1873 to 9 Highgate.

In 1816 a Kendal branch of a savings bank was opened which had its origins in a 'female benefit club' started in Tottenham in 1798 by Priscilla Wakefield. Her family, the Bells, were well-known Quakers and it was through their banking connections that she met and married Edward Wakefield after he migrated from Kendal to make a career in the south of England. The Kendal branch closed down in the 1890s, unable to cope with competition from the recently created Post Office Savings Bank. A plaque dated 1897 on the corner of Dowker Lane tells that 'Abbot Hall Public Pleasure Ground [was] acquired at the instance of the Directors of the Old Bank for Savings who contributed handsomely towards the cost'.

Building Societies

The earliest of the building societies of the type referred to previously were established in Birmingham and Leeds in the 1770s and 1780s. Later, the trend was taken up in Lancashire, Westmorland and Cumberland, the first probably formed in Preston in 1793. These early societies were mutual organisations made up of mainly working class members to respond to their housing needs. They were 'terminating societies' in the sense that they were wound up once the fund built up from members' regular subscriptions was sufficiently large to finance the building of a house for each share-holding member. So it was that, once the Kendal Union Building Society had built the 84 houses for its members and its affairs had been put in order, the society closed in 1830.

Another society, the Kendal Union New Building Society formed in 1825, was unsuccessful in achieving its aims. A general economic downturn and a depression in the local economy so inhibited the Society's Committee that they deferred the implementation of their plans to build houses once sufficient funds had been accumulated. In the intervening period funds dwindled as members sold back their shares to the Society. The upshot was that no houses were ever built by this Society.

A further underlying factor when comparing the fortunes of the two societies was the town's population which grew more quickly between 1811 and 1821 than in any other ten year period between 1801 and 1851. In the years from 1818 to the early 1820s there was a strong revival in building activity in England as the uncertainties of the Napoleonic War receded. This was the pattern in Kendal where businessmen such as Gandy were involved in major building development near the Green and at Longpool. The Kendal Union New Building Society was launched too late to catch this tide of economic growth and property development.

Thereafter terminating building societies were gradually replaced by permanent organisations, a change reflected in the name of many societies established in the forty years after the Kendal Union Building Society had been terminated. An example is the Kendal and Northern Counties

Permanent Benefit Building Society 'established under the provisions of an Act made in the 6th and 7th years of William IV intituled (sic) 'An Act for the Regulation of Benefit Building Societies".

Three of those involved in building houses on the Green in the early years, referred to later, are known to have taken out mortgages with this society: Messrs. Rigg and Burnett in relation to 4 and 5 Albert Road East, and John Robinson for *1–3 Fairfield*. Burnett had fifteen shares in the society which entitled him to an advance of £300 whereas Robinson's mortgage amounted to £1,100 against his holding of 55 shares. In all three cases those who signed on behalf of the society were William Wakefield, banker, and Isaac Whitwell Wilson and Charles Lloyd Braithwaite 'the younger', both manufacturers. As noted in Chapter 5, all these were Kendal Fell Trustees at various points in time after 1862.

CHAPTER II

BUILDING DEVELOPMENT ON KENDAL GREEN[†]

THREE SOURCES OF LAND

WE TURN NOW to the house building which took place in the immediate area of the Green on land from three sources. The most important was that part of Kendal Fell called 'Low Tenter Fell', consisting of all those plots of land not named on the extract shown overleaf from John Watson's 1847 map of the whole of the Fell lands. All houses on the west side of the Green from No. 7 up to and including No. 30 were built on Low Tenter Fell as were those on the east side from 48 to 65, excluding the four houses, Empson Hill, Hillside, Thorncroft and Zenith.

These houses were built on land from the second source, made up of two plots shown on the 1847 map as owned by Edward William Wakefield, half way up the east side of the Green. In the 1950s and 1960s when the houses were built the land was owned by Wavell Wakefield, 'Lord Wakefield of Kendal' who inherited it from his grandfather, William Wakefield, 1825–1893 via Wavell's father, Edward William Wakefield, 1799–1858.

The six terrace houses, 1–6 Kendal Green, originally called *Wood Lea*, were built on the other plot of Wakefield land, owned by William Wakefield. In 1847 it was shown as being owned by Edward William Wakefield who had inherited the land from Jacob Wakefield. Then, on Edward's death in 1858, the land passed to his son William.

Nine years later William sold for £30–16s–0d some 352 square yards of the plot – lying behind 16 & 18 Green Road and described as part of 'Bell

† In this chapter the original road and house names and numbering are used. In brackets are shown the modern numbering (e.g. 24 KG)

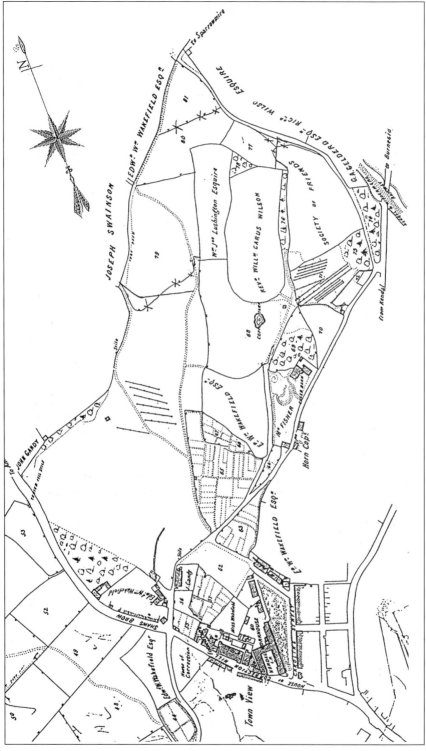

This extract from the 1847 Kendal Fell Lands map shows the area of Low Tenter Fell on which Kendal Green was created. The owners of plots of land not administered by the Fell Trust are named.

Parrock' – to William Hutchinson who owned the houses. A covenant was agreed as part of the sale that required Hutchinson to take down part of the garden wall and to remove the gate on the corner of Green Road and Kendal Green. It also permitted Wakefield and his 'heirs and assigns... or their servants agents tenants workmen friends or others to pass and repass over' what, in effect, was the garden in front of the houses. To this day the rights still stand as does the gate in the wall to the west of the garden through which Wakefield and his nominees were allowed to troop.[1] This clause is repeated in the deeds of houses in *Wood Lea*.

The third piece of land was that accumulated by the architect William Alfred Nelson leading up to his own house, *Holmfield*. Over a period of many years the houses numbered 36 to 49 were built on this plot.

There are no houses numbered 31 to 35 on the Green presumably because, when the roads were renamed *Kendal Green* in 1941, space was left for five houses on the Fell land taken up eventually by the playing field of St. Thomas' School.

In Appendix 1 are listed some of the key pieces of information on all of the houses now numbered or named on Kendal Green. This contains most or all of the information known about many of the houses which are therefore not referred to in the remainder of this chapter. There we concentrate on other houses about which more is known, mainly those constructed in the fifty years between the 1861 Act and 1911 all shown on an OS map published in the latter year. Later in the chapter we refer to other houses built after that period including those inserted into the gaps left around the main part of the Green, others built as an extension to the Green to the north-east and, finally, the Underley Estate and St. Thomas' school.

Appendix 2 consists of a summary of the census information for Kendal Green for the years 1871, 1881, 1891 and 1901. From the tables shown there it is possible to identify early residents (who are not necessarily the owners) of houses built by those dates and to track changes during the thirty year period.

THE FIRST FIFTY YEARS, 1861–1911

In a published list of 'events that changed the face of Kendal in the nineteenth century' the only mention of the Green refers to 1884 which saw the 'construction of the west side of Kendal Green'.[2] In fact the first building started in 1864 so that by 1884 eight houses had been completed on

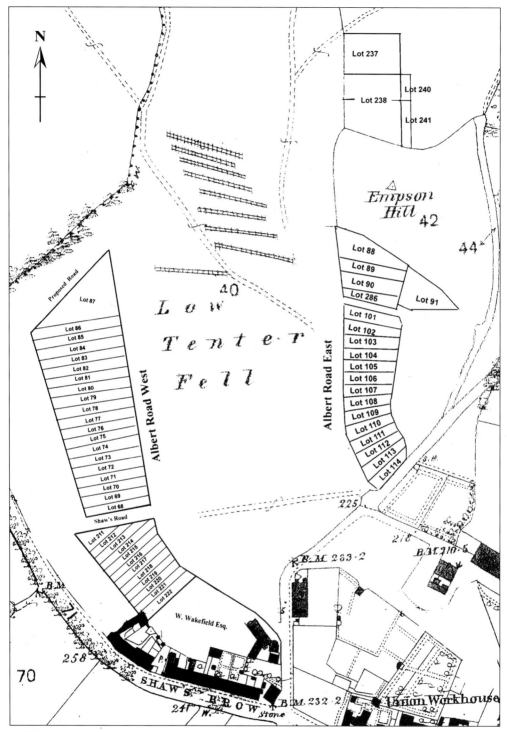

Building plots offered at auction by Kendal Fell Trust, drawn on map of Low Tenter Fell

Albert Road East and a terrace of three at *Fairfield* on the west side of the Green. Among these are some very fine dwellings.

The first building activity followed from several auctions of Kendal Fell lands held in 1861 and 1862. However, it is clear from the stipulations attached to the sale that these were not intended for workers with incomes similar to those who were provided with houses by Kendal Union Building Society in the 1820s. Whereas the cost of each of their houses was approximately £80, the early contracts between the Fell Trust and the purchasers of Kendal Green plots required the latter to build houses of at least £400 in value.

Building plots were offered for sale by the Trustees in various parts of the Fell lands including Greenside and Queen's Road. Plans were drawn up by the Trust's surveyor for each area showing numbered plots. Those for the north of the town showed several hundred plots on both sides of Kendal Green, Airethwaite, Ferney Green, Green Road, Crook Lea off House of Correction Hill, Shaw's Brow and further along what was then called the 'Kendal and Ambleside Turnpike Road'. The land on Kendal Green was all south of where St Thomas' school was built later, covering plots occupied by houses now numbered 1 to 30 on the west side and 50 to 65 to the east.

The main roads shown on the plan produced by the Trustees are Albert Road West, from Green Road and round the top of the Green where it joined up with Albert Road East, running down to join Horncop Lane. The name was chosen to commemorate the death of Prince Albert in December 1861.

An analysis of records of when the 51 plots of land on Low Tenter Fell were sold reveals considerable fluctuations as between ten-year periods as shown in the following table:

TABLE 1

Period	No. of Sales
1861–1870	18
1871–1880	1
1881–1890	24
1891–1900	8

These fluctuations may have resulted from economic trends in employment and building similar to those referred to in the introduction when discussing the different fortunes of the two Kendal terminating building societies. Unfortunately we have no evidence on how such issues affected workers in Kendal during the period 1861 to 1899 but national data shows periods of falling prices after 1873 to which employers responded by laying workers off. As a result, levels of unemployment fluctuated significantly, rising to a peak in the years 1879 and 1886.[3]

Building on the Green started soon after the first sales but it is difficult to date when houses were completed in every case, even when deeds are available, since while some were occupied by the original purchaser a significant proportion had tenants. In the latter case no sale transaction is recorded. So in the following attempt to list the houses in chronological order the date of sale of the land and/or the entry in the planning records are the main criteria, where available.

Apart from information about planning consent, building and completion, and some information about owners, especially early ones, a brief note is included on architectural features.

The position of houses on the Green can be identified by reference to the extract from the 1911 OS map opposite on which the present day numbering of some houses is shown.

1–3 Albert Road East (63–65 KG)

The first entry in the planning records, dated July 1864, refers to three houses to be erected for John Birkett, by G. Rigg, joiner. These were numbers 1 to 3 Albert Road East with the date-stone showing *JB, 1864* on the gable end of No. 1, overlooking Horncop Lane. On some plans the group of houses is called 'Denmark Terrace'.

In the auction of Fell land Birkett made the best bid, of £62-10s-8d, for lots 112, 113 and 114, described as 'part of the enclosure called Lower Tenter Fell'. In the deeds for 2 Albert Road East he was called on 'to build a dwelling house within 5 years' and to 'make and maintain the frontage'. Birkett is still registered as the owner of all three properties in 1874, each of which had a tenant.

Denmark Terrace

This is a very simple terrace typical of Kendal of that period with little extra decoration and no dormers. A string course runs under the upper

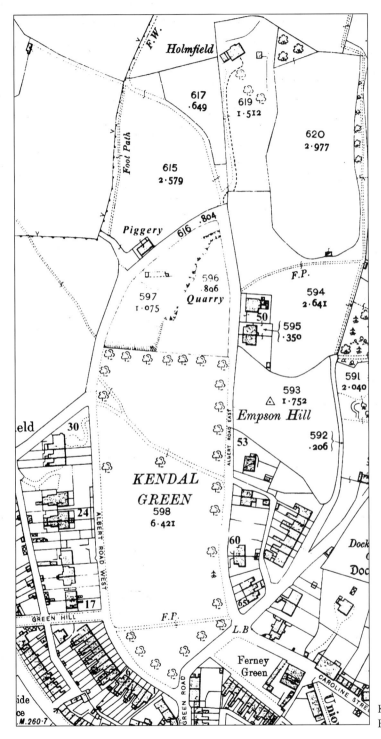

Kendal Green
Extract from 1911 OS map

windows across the terrace. Very shallow eaves are supported by small blocks in Georgian style but set further apart than would have been the practice in that period. Only No. 1 (65 KG) has original Kendal three pane sash windows. The doors seem narrow within quite formal surrounds, including a pediment over the lintel supported by an elaborate bracket of the sort for which designs would be available in builders' pattern books. There is interesting sculpting around bay windows but it does not continue across the broad pillars.

Datestone on gable end of No. I Albert Road East

The house (62 KG) added to the north end of the terrace in the 1930s is of a later style (see appendix I).

6–7 *Albert Road East* (*54–55 KG*)

Plans for two semi-detached houses were agreed in September 1865 for construction by the builder G. Rigg on this site for Messrs. Gaskell and Burrows. Rigg was shown as architect. The underlying design of the houses is similar to the terrace, Nos. 1 to 3, but changes made to the bay windows of both houses, and the dormer added to No. 6, tend to obscure the similarity.

4–5 *Albert Road East* (*60–61 KG*)

Messrs G. Rigg – shown as architect – and W.J. Burnett were granted planning approval on 4th December 1866 to build this pair of semi-detached

Albert Road East from path across Kendal Green showing Nos. 6–7 with Denmark House to the left.

houses. Their design is symmetrical at the front: matching doorways in the middle flanked by handsome bay windows with interesting moulding and four first floor windows set above doors and bays. There were no dormers in the original houses. Deep eaves are supported by five cast iron brackets probably of standard design. Stone arches over upper windows with mortar bands below create an impression of a continuous surround. A string course runs below upper windows, uniting the elevations. The doorways have quite elaborate pediments supported by standard design brackets; above is a fanlight with curved corners.

Each house has an extended side piece with its own chimneys and a lower window with lintel sitting on dressed stone blocks.

The Kendal Fell Trustees named in the deeds are George Foster Braithwaite, Samuel Rhodes, Thomas Busher and John Hudson.

There is however an anomaly in the documents for these two houses which, though semi-detached, are shown in the two sets of deeds as being built separately on land that – both agree – was bought originally by George Rigg. The sequence of events recorded started on 1st October 1866 with an announcement of the sale of lots 103 to 111 inclusive. Then, in December 1866, a planning application for two dwelling houses was agreed, presented jointly by Messrs. Rigg and Burnett. In both sets of deeds, Rigg, carpenter and joiner, is revealed as a successful bidder at an auction held in the Town Hall in 1867, purchasing lots 107 to 111.

However, the deeds of No. 5, apart from confirming Rigg's purchase in 1866 of plots 107 to 111, contain an indenture of 4th March 1867 recording the conveyance by Kendal Fell Trustees of 4,860 sq. yds. of land to William James Burnett a commercial clerk. A plan shows Burnett having acquired lots 107 and 108 with Rigg owning lot 109 and a William Thompson owning lot 106 on the north side. Signatories for the Trust were John Whitwell, Thomas Busher, John Fisher and John Farrer.

There is, however, no document showing any transfer back from Rigg to the Trust of his title to lots 107 & 108.

'Denmark House', 8 Albert Road East (53 KG)

The main area of land fronting Kendal Green on which this house stands was bought by Robert Butterwith as three lots from the Fell Trustees at an

auction in 1867. In the previous
year the planning records show
he sought permission for a
house to be built on this site by
G. Rigg.

The house is built four-
square, of a quite classical
design that preceded the flurry
of Victorian elaboration.
Chimneys are buttressed to the
front over a roof with deep
eaves, with strong return to sides, supported by strong but simple brackets. Stucco on the upper storey above a continuous string line adds interest. The three upper front windows, centred over bays and doorway, have
curved chiselled stone lintels supported on dressed stone blocks. The
stucco makes the windows more prominent but the painting out of the
lintels diminishes their effect.

Fine bays and doorway have no extraneous decoration. The bays are
supported on grand blocks of Urswick limestone.

On Butterwith's death in 1872 the property passed to his wife, Isabella,
and his brother Charles. They purchased an extra strip of land to the south
of the original plot. When Isabella died in 1919, Charles sold the property
to Albert Pickles who then bought two plots at the back of the existing
land which Richard Chorley, a solicitor living in Airethwaite Terrace, had
acquired in two separate purchases in the 1890s. One of these had been
acquired at an auction of Fell lands as early as 1864 by M. De Rome.

1–3 Fairfield (28–30 KG)

In August 1869 John Robinson, a painter and glazier, bought from the Fell
Trustees a parcel of land of 1,936 square yards on the 'west side and
fronting Kendal Green'. He was required to pay to the Trustees a perpetual
annual 'free farm rent' of £7-6s-0d.

On this land he built three houses in a terrace that is unusual in being
totally stuccoed, painted in a bright white which can be seen from Castle
Hill. Even so the strong regular quoins still stand out at the corners of the
terrace. A very full yet well-proportioned front aspect has bays that continue from ground to first floor set under narrow paired windows at attic
level. This 'modular arrangement' of the front of the terrace conceals the
different house sizes: No. 1 (30 KG) is a large double fronted house whereas
the other two are standard width. The dark framing of the windows and

doors stands out against the stucco walls. The paired attic windows with semi-circular heads are reminiscent of Webster.

As was typical of the early indentures by which such bargains were sealed a witness to Robinson's purchase signed an affidavit to confirm that the lands involved in the transaction had been part of Kendal Fell. In this case one Robert Shaw confirmed that to the best of his knowledge this had been so over a period of forty years.

At an auction at the Rainbow Inn on 8th June 1871 Robinson sold the three houses built on the site, the free farm rent being apportioned between them in proportion to their size. Henry Martindale, the County Treasurer, bought No. 3 *Fairfield* (28 KG) for £500 and Robinson retained No. 2 (29 KG) for his own use. Tenants occupied this house until 1889 when it was sold to Robert Benson Martindale.

The deeds do not reveal who purchased No. 1 (30 KG) but in the 1871 Census the head of the household was shown as Rachel Whitwell, 'living on the interest of money'. However, in the rate books of 1874 and 1884 Edward Whitwell is listed as owner-occupier, then in the 1891 Census as head of the household. By 1901 Rachel Whitwell was back in this role but the rate book of 1904 shows that, while she was the occupier, the house was owned by Edward Whitwell's executors. They were still the owners in 1924 when Mary Whitwell was the occupier. For at least the period from 1931 to 1936, however, she owned the house but let it to tenants.

Early in the 20th century the narrow road just beyond the house leading up to Windermere Road – now called Fairfield Lane – was known as Whitwell's Lane and some long-standing residents still call it that.

In 1948 planning permission to split *1 Fairfield* into three flats was granted to a Mr Rowling who lived at 7 Kendal Green.

A 1932 photograph of part of Albert Road West featuring 1 and 2 Fairbank, Laurel Mount and Holly Bank, Oakdene, and Silver Howe and Overdale (i.e. Nos. 17–24 Kendal Green, with a gap where No. 22, The Newlands was built in 1937)

Oakdene (21 KG)

Joseph Jordan, a corn merchant, bought two plots in June 1884, on which a large double-fronted house, *Oakdene*, was built, commemorated on its date stone inscribed *C & J, 1884* (Caroline and Joseph Jordan). It was designed by a well known Kendal architect, Stephen Shaw, who was responsible for many fine houses in the town.

Oakdene is itself a fine house with much interesting detail. The hipped roof and the two full gables, extending across three floors at the front, show typical Victorian skill in manipulating complex roof shapes. In its Mock Tudor decoration and the sculpted corners of the upper storey the house shows a more cosmopolitan influence than others around the Green. In this sense *Oakdene* leads into a modern architectural style. Perhaps the only disappointment is the door with a shallow five centre arch tucked under the balcony which seems to have constrained its design.

To the rear of the house were built stables and coach house, midden, earth closet, a room for dry ashes and a wash-house.

In 1885 the Kendal Fell Trustees agreed to a petition from Jordan to be allowed to buy a neighbouring plot that had been offered in 1864 but which he had not been able to afford then. He admitted that the extra land was needed for garden because he had built a larger house on the original plots than had at first been planned. In 1891 he bought a further plot, extending again the garden to the north side of the house as shown on the 1911 map.

In 1905 the reception for the wedding of Jordan's son, John – known as 'Jack' – was held at *Oakdene*. Among the guests were Stephen Shaw and family, including his son Malcolm and daughter Margaret.

In 1922 *Oakdene* was bought by David Dodds who had moved up from Kidderminster to revive carpet manufacture at the Highgate mill. His son George inherited *Oakdene* but decided to let it, and planning permission was obtained by architects Shaw and Smith to convert the house into three flats but the necessary work was never done.

Oakdene in 1932

A group at the wedding of Jack Jordan photographed in 1905 on the steps of Oakdene.

1 and 2 Fairbank (17–18 KG).

On the map of Kendal Green plots it was noted that those on which these houses were probably built were bought by Messrs Wiper, Hodgson and Levens in 1882. A planning application in the names of Mr & Mrs Wiper and W. Levens was agreed in June of that year.

As can be seen from the photograph earlier these houses are a well-balanced pair with deep eaves and fine bays but compared to *Oakdene* and the later terraces the roofs of the dormers have a somewhat shallow angle which diminishes their effect. One of the few decorative details is the patterning of the dormer barge boards. Presumably the repaired pediment over the left hand doorway reflects the original form and the other has been modified at some later date.

In 1884 and 1891 Robert Dixon, bacon curer, and David Pennington, general manager of an iron foundry, were owner-occupiers of *1 and 2 Fairbank* respectively.

Laurel Mount and Holly Bank (19–20 KG)

A planning application by Messrs. Wiper, Hodgson and Levens was agreed for this pair of houses in 1883. The exact date of building is not known but an 1885 Directory made reference to them.

With their steeper pitched dormers, the modelling of the attic windows and the double first-floor windows these houses present a more interesting front aspect than *Fairbank*. On the other hand the set-back wings in a shallow L-shaped plan leave an untidy roof line. The doors are framed quite generously with arched lintel over double lights.

Laurel Mount changed hands between 1885 and 1891 being occupied by William Allwood, commercial traveller on the first date and Alfred Grayson, registered dentist on the later one.

James Singleton, Assistant to HM Inspector of Schools, lived in *Holly Bank* (20 KG) in 1885 and 1891.

Highfield (50 KG)

Highfield is a four-square house built on the corner of what is now Empsom Road. It has a straight-pitched roof with chimney stacks at each end; like those at *Denmark House* these are buttressed to the front. The front of the house is of a very different construction from the sides, with uneven courses of dark stone between dressed stone quoins, string course and bay windows. The sides of the house are in random limestone with much less uniform quoins to the back.

Three first floor windows are centred over bays and a front door which

are sheltered by an extended porch under a shallow pitched roof and returned ends. The string course follows the line of this roof and then stops at the end of the front wall. All windows and the top of the very simple door frame have unusual tightly curved upper corners that seem somewhat out of place.

A planning application by a Mr Lyon for this house was agreed in July 1880, to be built by a Mr Thompson. In the 1904 Rate Book George Lyon is shown as *Highfield's* owner-occupier, described as 'painter, gilder, glazier, picture frame maker, and dealer in oils, paints, colours etc'.[4] He lived there until at least 1906.

1 and 2 Fern Lea (51–52 KG)

These semi-detached houses have a half depth extension at the side to a shallow L-shape plan. However, within this overall plan they are arranged asymmetrically in that the bay window of the left-hand house is set to the left and the main door to the right of it with half-moon light over, whereas the bay of the other house is centred so that the main door, with squarish light above, is crushed into the front of the narrow extension.

In contrast the two dormers and four first floor windows, all with lightly curved lintels, are set symmetrically within the front elevation. The dormer pitch is quite shallow with an unusual notch at the peak.

Deeds for *1 Fern Lea (52 KG)* show that the house has had only four owners, including the present ones, since it was first sold in 1884. The land was bought by William Simpson as two separate plots in June 1880 and

July 1882 and he sold *1 Fern Lea* to Margaret and Sarah Watson in September 1884 for £730. Margaret Watson died in 1934 and Sarah in 1939 when it was sold for £915 by her executor to Ada and Edith Stubbs who died in 1977 and 1989 respectively.

It is assumed that the two houses were built together and that *2 Fern Lea* was also sold at about the same time as its neighbour. In 1884 John Illingworth, tobacco manufacturer, was the owner-occupier of the house listed as *Fern Lea* (assumed to be No. 2) but in the 1891 census Catherine Illingworth, widow, had become head of the household.

1–6 Wood Lea† (1–6 KG)

The name of this terrace, and *Beechwood* immediately beyond it, derive from a triangular woodland shown on the 1847 Fell Lands map between Windermere Road and the Green. The six houses of *Wood Lea* and the ten of *Beechwood* give a strong sense of unity to Kendal Green's architecture especially as they are likely to be the first houses seen by most people entering the area coming as they mainly do from Green Road, Caroline Street or Horncop Lane.

In 1880 William Wakefield applied for planning permission to build on the land he still owned on this site after his sale of the small plot to Hutchinson. No further information has been found on what happened to this application but, five years later, on 11th February 1885 the land was conveyanced from Wakefield to William Levens, Builder and Carpenter of Ferney Green, and Martin Hodgson, Mill Manager, who paid £240-12s-6d in equal shares. It was they who, in March of that year, were granted planning approval to build *Wood Lea*, 'six houses on a plot of land behind Shaw's Brow and facing Kendal Green'. Levens was shown as the architect.

The detail of the terrace, including quite sharply peaked attic dormers, is typical of a confident Victorian style at work in a group of houses which seem clearly designed as a unit. This is shown most markedly in the double-windowed attics at each end of the terrace that act as 'book-ends'. This may also have been the reason for the extra inverted 'T' frame within the dormer roof of No. 6 but, if so, its mirror structure in No. 1 has been destroyed at some time. The doorframes comprise an attractive arch with half-moon lights above the doors.

A slightly different orientation of the next terrace, *Beechwood*, allows 6 *Wood Lea* to be extended to about half the depth of the house, filling part of the wedge shaped gap between the terraces.

Some measure of the initial value of the houses is revealed in the sale of No. 3 to Edward Todd in May 1886 for £425 and No. 6 to James Ruthven in November 1887 for £590. The difference in a year is surprising especially in the light of Todd's sale in 1890 of No. 3 for only £435.

---

† Though the address of some of the houses in this terrace, including No. 3, is *Wood Lea* for others it is *Wood Leigh* or even *Woodleigh* as used in the 1891 Census

Wood Lea & Beechwood Terrace

1–10 *Beechwood Terrace* (7–16 KG)

Hodgson and Levens were granted permission on 8th March 1886 for 'ten houses to be called Beechwood to be built in a plantation facing Kendal Green'. Again Levens was shown as architect. Hodgson was the highest bidder for land of area 3,102½ square yards sold at auction by the Kendal Fell Trustees on 27th May 1886 for which he paid £762-14s-0d. An indenture of 30th April 1887 prescribed that eleven houses were to be built by William Levens, the value of each to be not less than £400. The eleventh house referred to is Beechwood Cottage on Green Hill. The purchasers agreed to meet ¹⁄₁₀ of the cost of drains and ¹⁄₁₁ of half of the cost of the back lane (i.e. shared with other Beechwood Terrace houses and Beechwood Cottage on their side of the lane and houses on Shaw's Brow also backing onto the lane).

The basic design of this terrace is very similar to *Wood Lea* with single dormer windows set over double first floor windows centred above the bay. However, in this case the large expanse of wall between first floor windows is broken by a single first-floor window over each door. There is more detailing too, for example, in the chamfered window lintels and the keystones in the doorframe arch. The double-attic windows and inverted-T-framed dormers for Nos. 1 and 10 provide symmetrical book-ends for this terrace. Somewhere in its middle section the row of houses is cranked slightly to allow it to follow the curve of the road

Despite the apparent quality of this terrace and *Wood Lea* their construction is typical of 'spec-built' narrow frontage terrace houses of any era with the party walls supporting the floors, allowing the internal walls to be in cheaper timber stud work.

No. 8 was sold to George Haywood, grocer, and his wife, Isabella, on 30th April 1887 for £460. On 2nd May 1919 Isabella Haywood paid 10 shillings to George Haywood for conveyance of the property to her and the release of his claim to possession; he admitted that she paid the full sum for the house originally from her own money.

The deeds for *10 Beechwood* show that it was sold to Vincent Salvator Smith on 30th April 1887, although its date stone is inscribed *VS & ES, 1886* (i.e. the date the land was purchased). The initials ES are those of his wife, Emily.

Silver Howe & Overdale (23–24 KG)

This pair of semi-detached houses and the neighbouring ones, *Holly Croft*, were built on part of a plot of land which Kendal Fell Trustees sold to Martin Hodgson in May 1899. The plot extended from the northern boundary of the garden of *Oakdene* (21 KG) to the wall of *3 Fairfield Terrace* (28 KG) an area of 3,943 square yards.

Hodgson was contracted to build ten dwelling houses to the value of £550 each within four years. Only two months after acquiring the plot Hodgson obtained the Trustees' agreement to build only nine houses, claiming that he needed to allow a yard at each end of the site. In fact, the

site as purchased was only just long enough to have accommodated a terrace of nine houses of similar dimensions to those in Beechwood Terrace which Hodgson and Levens had constructed thirteen years earlier.

Two years later in May 1902 Hodgson attempted to persuade the Trustees to vary the conditions of sale yet again, arguing that the class of houses he had envisaged building in his initial application were no longer required. Under pressure from the Trustees he clarified that he now intended to build three pairs of semi-detached houses on the site, valued at £650 or more each. This was agreed but, in the event, Hodgson built only two pairs of semi-detached houses, now numbers 23/24 and 25/26 Kendal Green. So, in June 1913 the Borough Council, which had taken over Kendal Fell Trust's duties six years earlier, reacquired the remaining land noting that it should be used 'only for the construction of dwelling houses or a gymnasium'!

The architect for *Silver Howe* and *Overdale* was Hodgson's son, Arthur Nicholas Whitfield Hodgson, aged 22 in 1902, the year in which the plans were approved. The houses were completed by 1904. Their bays extend up into the first floor with vertical division of the main window pane at both levels. Above them are wide three-bay second floor windows under quite deep gabled eaves supported by regular brackets and a pediment at each end.

The space between the gables is taken up at ground floor with adjoining doorways flanked by pillars supporting a balcony joining the two first floor bays, a northern version of Queen Anne Revival styling. The balcony is set in a deep and somewhat high recess up to the horizontal stretch of roof connecting the gables. Visible at the back of each balcony is a door with side windows and, above, a semi-circular multi-paned window.

The elevated position of these houses and others to the north of it on the west side of the Green allowed quite grand approaches to be constructed.

In August 1904 Charles Fildes became the first tenant of *Overdale*. In the previous year a planning application was agreed for a bicycle shed, perhaps to house Fildes' motor and pedal tricycles.[5]

No. 24 Kendal Green was saved from substantial modification threatened by a planning application submitted in 1951 by the company, Isaac Braithwaite & Son, who had bought the house in that year. Their proposal to convert it into two flats was withdrawn after only three months and the house was eventually sold again in 1962 at a small loss. During those years the house was occupied by Norman Turvey, company secretary for Braithwaites (Drysalters).

For many years *Silver Howe* was occupied by tenants, and was still owned by Hodgson's executors in 1936. The first tenant was a Mrs Eliza Brown who lived there from at least 1906 to 1910.

Holly Croft (25–26 KG)

This is the name given to what were planned as two semi-detached houses. Martin Hodgson obtained planning permission to build them in 1905 to a design by his son Arthur. However, they were used as one house at least from 1910 when Isaac Braithwaite was listed as occupier and Hodgson the owner. The joint use of the two houses seems to be confirmed by the 1911 OS map which shows no separate front gardens; instead the area to the front opens into the unused plot of land to the north on which the third pair of houses should have been built, already laid out with a drive winding into the back lane.

Though built by the same developer as *Silver Howe* and *Overdale* the roof design of this pair of houses is significantly different comprising two large gables in a more 'Arts and Crafts' style with long eaves capping the gable ends in a very definite pediment. The main windows in the two storey bay are in one section only. Originally a cosmetic balcony was set above the porch, supported by columns similar to that in the next houses; it presumably gave some sort of balance to the elevation. The offset second floor venetian windows with a half-moon projection above the main lintel are typical Queen Anne Revival features.

On 11th May 1914 Mrs Mary Snowden Braithwaite bought Nos. 25 and 26 – described then in the deeds as 'Holly Croft, formerly two houses' – and the land beyond which had been previously owned by Hodgson.

In 1910 a school for girls run on Quaker principles was opened at *Holly Croft* by Kathleen Mary Wilson. Three years later a planning application was submitted to join together the two pairs of semi-detached houses, 23/24 (*Silver Howe and Overdale*) and 25/26 (*Holly Croft*) to form one large school.

The following year a much less radical proposal was submitted for planning approval showing only a large glazed cover over the back yard between the two pairs of houses. There is no sign around the properties now that even this limited alteration was made and it seems that the school closed in 1914. In both pairs of houses, however, there are clear signs of where they had been joined internally at ground and first floor levels in the positions indicated in the 1913 planning application.

This feature may have been useful later when, during the First World War, the two pairs of houses were used to house Belgian refugees, the last of whom left Kendal to return home in 1919. At some point in this period *Holly Croft* became a home for unmarried mothers, supervised by Edith Peach, and was renamed *St. Monica's*. The house was used for this purpose until the early 1930s.

In the 1938 Electoral Register it had been split into two dwellings, listed as *1 and 2 Holly Croft.*

Holmfield (41 KG)

This large detached house in its own grounds stands on the edge of a steep slope facing north towards Potter Fell, at the north-eastern corner of what is now Kendal Green. It was built by William Alfred Nelson for his own use at the far end of a large plot of land he and his brother Edward bought in 1904, as noted earlier. The land extended down almost as far as where Empsom Road is now, all shown on the 1847 Kendal Fell lands map as belonging to a William Lushington.

The house is very exotic in the Kendal setting in its complete departure from the local pattern of style and materials. Immediately one notices the distinctive mansard roof in red tiles topped by chimney stacks with double string lines. The floor plan of the house produces a very complex roof structure. First floor windows set into the steeply sloping sides are shallow dormers below which the roof kicks out sharply to deep lower eaves. Windows in end walls are protected by similarly deep eaves which give a 'bonnet' effect to those elevations. Lintels of ground floor windows are tucked under the lower eaves. The twin-windowed main door is flanked by slightly lower windows; spanning them all are three small windows above the door and larger ones to the side.

It is assumed that Nelson, a local architect, designed the house. If so, he seems to have borrowed a Dutch style of domestic architecture for its main structure. As for the internal details – such as the panelled inglenook and fine mantelpiece and pierglass – he is said to have been influenced by Hugh Baillie Scott who designed the grand house *Blackwell* (1897–1900) overlooking Windermere, opened to the public in 2001. Although plans for *Holmfield* were agreed in 1905 the date carved into a wooden arch above an inglenook in the dining room was 1904.

On 23rd December 1924 Nelson sold the house to Samuel Gawith his son-in-law, a snuff and tobacco manufacturer, who lived there with his family until 1954.

To this point we have dealt with what is known of the 39 houses shown on the 1911 map – 22 terraced, 12 semi-detached and 5 detached, including *Holly Croft* as one house. Of these all but five are built totally of limestone showing on all faces; the exceptions are *Holmfield* and *Nos. 1–3 Fairfield* which are stuccoed and *Highfield*, where the front is in a dark stone. All except *Holmfield* are roofed in slate. Most of the houses have cellars and generous accommodation which, in many cases, is spread over three floors.

Eleven were listed in the 1871 Census (including two uninhabited at that time, at 'Fairfield Villas', and three under construction) the same as are listed as complete on the 1881 Census. By 1891 the total had risen to 35 of which one was unoccupied. The same number of houses are listed in 1901. In 1910 the rates and valuation records show that only 18 (46%) of the 39 houses were owner occupied, the other 21 were rented.

BUILDING POST-1911

In this section we deal only with those houses, built in the remaining gaps on the main part of the Green, about which some interesting information has been discovered over and above what is summarised in Appendix 1.

The Newlands (22 KG)

George Dodds, the son of David Dodds who had purchased *Oakdene* from Jordan in 1922, was proposing to marry in March 1937 his fiancée Dorothy, daughter of the Blacows who lived at *Laurel Mount* (19 KG). So in March of the previous year they started planning the construction of a house in the garden of *Oakdene* to be paid for by his father. An architect, Malcolm Shaw, was consulted about the design and after many modifications to the early plans a double-fronted house was decided upon, to be built in rendered brick. Various builders gave estimates and advice about placing the house on the sloping plot in ways that would reduce the expense of construction and ensure that it was not built too near *Oakdene*.

In March 1937 planning permission was granted and construction started on a level site, cut into the slope, well above the road. Its front garden was set out below, incorporating an existing south-facing summer house; a gate connected its path to *Oakdene*. Various greenhouses and sheds formed part of the rear garden. The house and external work was completed in October 1937.

Pinewoods (27 KG)

The plot of land bought by Hodgson in 1899 – on which according to his agreement with the Fell Trust he should have built a third pair of semi-detached houses – was put up for auction by the Corporation in 1933. It was bought for £225 by Ronald Pickles, son of Albert Pickles of *Denmark House*, on which he and his fiancée Alice Metcalf planned to build *Pinewoods* to live in after their marriage. Together they organised its design and construction with the help of a local architect, John Dyson, such that the shell was completed in November 1934 and finished off a few months before their wedding in September 1935. The total cost of the house was £1,545 and further amounts of £470 and £350 respectively were spent on laying out the garden and furnishing the interior.

Empson Hill

When David and Eileen Russell were planning a family house on Empson Hill in the early 1960s, the company in which he was a partner was beginning to develop an estate of houses in the hollow to the north between Kendal Green and Prickley Fell. The company commissioned E. Donald Haigh Architects (now Haigh Architects) to design a range of 'mini' and normal bungalows and two-storey houses of various sizes to be arranged in several different configurations along what was to be Empsom Road, looping around the valley floor.

The Russells also asked Michael Bottomley, the architect involved in this development, to design a modern house for them on Empson Hill. The Russells submitted an application to build in the dip to the north of the summit, a proposal which was agreed subject to the house not obscuring the view of *1 Fern Lea* (52 KG) from the planning office located in town. A profile showing the shape of the building was erected on the site to show the height of the house when built, allowing the planners to check that it would not interrupt the sight line. To achieve this, a single storey house was designed, with a large cellar and a flat roof which, since it slopes into the centre of the main living area from east and west, is described as a 'butterfly roof'.

When building was started there were no trees on the hill and the Russells planted all of the trees now growing there to attract birds and other wild life.

David and Eileen Russell and their two children moved into their new home just before Christmas 1964; their third child was born there. They called the house *Empson Hill* to match the name of the area on the OS maps whereas the County Council decided to call the nearby road Empsom Road.[6]

Nos. 56–59 Kendal Green

In 1868 four plots were sold by the Trustees to William Thompson for £97-5s-2d but the land was not built on and changed hands several times over the subsequent years. It ended up the property of a builder, William Dixon, who obtained planning permission in 1922 to build a terrace of four houses on the site, abutting but not joined to Nos. 54 and 55. The Rates Book for 1924 lists two of the four houses, without numbers, but shows no owners.

Finally, we deal with buildings constructed at the north end of the Green including the houses built on the land accumulated by Alfred Nelson, the Underley Estate and St Thomas' school. All except *Holmfield*, already described, were built after 1911.

The land owned by Alfred Nelson started with the plot he and his brother Edward acquired jointly in 1904, on which Alfred's house *Holmfield* was built. The deeds of the house refer to a will made by James Wilson in 1801 in which he bequeathed to his daughter Barbara 'freehold

View from the edge of the golf course down to Underley and the houses to the north-east of the main part of the Green. St Thomas' School is to the left.

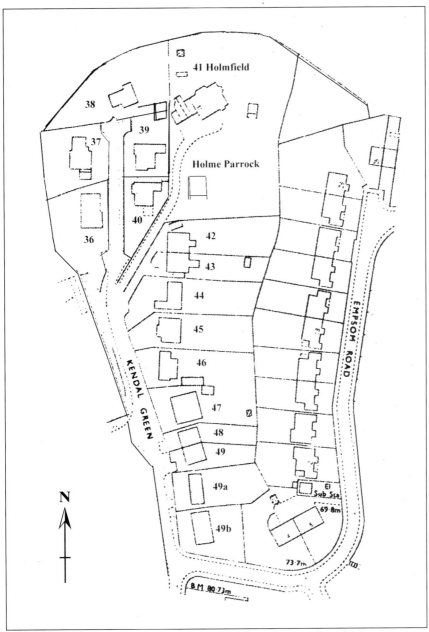

Sketch map of the area of land to the north-east of the main part of Kendal Green on which houses Nos. 36 to 49b were built.

land called Holme Parrock on the Tenter Fell'. She married W. J. Lushington who died in 1845, the name shown against that plot of land on the 1847 map.

After Barbara's death in 1858 a large set of beneficiaries sold the land to William Slee. He died in 1889 leaving a will that instructed his wife and two friends, Richard Bownass and Gilbert Hayhurst, to sell the land and 'convert into money' as soon as convenient.

Hayhurst died in 1886 and Mrs Slee in 1904 after which Bownass sold the land to Edward and Alfred Nelson. In 1907 Edward Nelson sold out his interest in the property to Alfred, an architect, who had by then already made several attempts to obtain outline planning permission for various houses on the land, most of which, if not all, were turned down.

Then in 1924 Nelson swapped with Kendal Borough Council some land he owned in Sedbergh Road for land near *Holmfield*, originally administered by the Kendal Fell Trust but by then owned by the Council. The land the Council transferred to Nelson was in two parts, the larger being the triangular plot between the land he already owned and the Kendal Fell land numbered 79 on which St Thomas' School was later built. The plot acquired included an area described in the indenture as 'potato ground'. Then there was a smaller, almost square piece of an area called 'Tarn Close', immediately south of his own land. A small tarn, Copt Tarn, is shown on the 1847 Fell Lands map.

North-east extension of the Green

Over a period of time housing plots and the roads to service them were laid across the three areas of land owned by Nelson, including part of that acquired with Edward Nelson in 1904. The resulting area of land, and plans of the houses built on it is shown on the sketch map on the previous page. Some of the information known about the houses and their occupants is contained in the summary listing in Appendix 1 and in Chapter 6, which deals with people who lived on the Green.

Underley and St. Thomas' School

Two adjoining plots of land are still unaccounted for at the top of the Green. The more easterly of the two was triangular in shape owned initially by the Kendal Fell Trust and then, after 1907, the Kendal Corporation. In its south-west corner was a small solitary building, part of a piggery associated with the Workhouse. Between this plot and Fairfield Lane was a much larger area of land also fronting the Green. On the 1862 map of the Fell plots for sale, a Mary Harrison was shown as its owner.

Opening ceremony of second phase of Underley Estate

It was on this latter site that planning permission was granted in July 1913 to the Kendal Co-Partnership Housing Society to build 24 'workmen's houses' designed by J. Stalker on '2 stiles field'. They were laid out as six pairs of semi-detached houses and four short terraces of four forming a shallow crescent joining Kendal Green next to Fairfield Lane at one end and the Corporation plot of land at the other. The work was started by Martindales the builders but as their employees were called up to do military service Dixons helped out. The development was named Underley Avenue after Lord Henry Bentinck of Underley Hall, Kirkby Lonsdale, who played a leading part locally in creating public housing for working people.

There was a post-war depression nation-wide as, from 1921 on, demand for goods and services slumped and unemployment increased sharply. Not until 1926 was a start made on extending the Underley Estate when, in March of that year, a planning application was agreed for the building of '48 semi-detached cottages adjacent to 2 stiles field'. The joint applicants were the architects G. Morland and M. G. Shaw on behalf of Kendal Co-Partnership Housing Society Ltd., the builders were J. W. Howie of Bridge Street. Two different designs were employed, one used for 40 of the houses provided for a bathroom off the scullery, while the other, used for only 8 houses, had the bathroom upstairs. The completed houses were set out along Underley Road – leading from Underley Avenue to join up with Windermere Road – and Underley Hill, a circular crescent off this road. The houses were completed between 27th August 1926 and 30th January 1928.

The one other virgin site still fronting the Green, owned by the Corporation after 1907, was not developed until 1966 when it was used to re-house St Thomas' School. As part of the preparation of the site the piggery was demolished and some of its timbers incorporated into a shed in the garden of 30 Underley Avenue just across from where the piggery had stood.

CHAPTER III

OTHER LOCAL DEVELOPMENT FROM 1861

SCHOOLS: KENDAL GREEN & AIRETHWAITE

BY THE LATE 1860s Low Tenter Fell and the surrounding area was changing considerably. Queen's Road was built in 1869 and by the time of the 1871 Census thirty-seven houses had been built on Kendal Fell Trust lands to the north of the town including eleven on Kendal Green, nine on Woodside Terrace (Windermere Road), seven at Airethwaite and five in Green Road. Some 34 children of school age lived there, placing pressure on the schooling provision in this part of Kendal where the only day school was that run by the 'Stricklandgate Wesleyans'. The school had been set up in the original chapel building erected in 1808 and by 1868 it provided basic education for 84 infants and 61 junior boys and 35 girls in cramped accommodation with hardly any playground. Considered a successful school it was popular in the area and children were being turned away regularly. Though plans for expansion were drawn up in an attempt to meet the extra demands on accommodation stemming from the 1870 Forster Education Act, it was decided these plans would not meet the need fully.[1]

So 'an influential meeting of gentlemen interested in Education was held in December 1870' from which stemmed a decision to build 'Kendal Green School' in the block between Caroline Street and House of Correction Hill to 'accommodate all the children in the district, not already provided for by the excellent Infant School connected with St. Thomas' Church'. The Trustees of the Wesleyan school agreed that their school would be closed down when the new one opened.

Although a recent Act had allowed for school boards to make a charge on the rates to fund the building of schools, no board was ever created in Kendal so the new school, like all others in the town, was maintained by public subscription. Hence a circular issued to raise subscriptions to pay for the new school notes that its erection as one of a series of 'British Schools'… 'will probably save the town the expense of a 'Board School'. So the philanthropy of those involved was somewhat double edged.[2]

The list of 98 subscribers included seventeen from the major Kendal Quaker families and five living on the Green in 1871 who subscribed directly or through their businesses: i.e. John Birkett, Butterwith & Son, George Gaskell, George Rigg and Edward Whitwell.

In February 1872 planning permission to build the school was given to a 'G. Rigg', presumably the George Rigg who built houses on the Green, lived in one of them and responded to the appeal for subscriptions.

When the school opened in July 1873, 181 children were registered, a number that increased to 272 three years later against a nominal capacity of 470. Following the appointment of William Gardiner as headmaster in 1884 pupil numbers increased significantly. This trend, together with a better appreciation of the requirements of the Forster Act, induced the school governors to make plans in early 1885 for carrying out extensive alterations to the school, 'rendered necessary by the increase in the number of scholars, and by the demands of the Education Department'. These demands included the phasing out of both the 'monitorial' system of teaching – whereby the more advanced students, called Monitors, taught the younger pupils – and the practice of using Pupil Teachers which had been introduced into Kendal Green School in 1873 after Monitors had been phased out.[3]

On Kendal Green alone the number of houses increased from nine in 1871 – two years before the new school was built – to 34 in 1891 and the corresponding number of children of school age rose from 5 to 31. The situation ten years later was little different. If the total numbers of houses built on local Kendal Trust lands between 1871 and 1891 matched this trend on the Green it is likely that about 115 houses would have been created with 105 children requiring school places.

October of 1895 heralded a major fundraising event – a 'Grand Oriental Bazaar: Constantinople in Kendal' – held in St. George's Hall over three days. The brochure tells us that, 'as the future of England depends upon the development of the characters of the children of today, their education should be conducted with the utmost care, and money spent for this purpose is spent, undoubtedly, supremely well'. The principal

OFFICIAL HANDBOOK

OF THE

Grand Oriental

Bazaar

TO BE HELD IN

St. George's Hall,

ON

OCT. 17, 18, 19, 1895.

G. M. BRIDGES
BAZAAR DECORATOR.
KINGS LYNN.

OFFICIAL HANDBOOK

"Know ye the land of the cedar and vine,
Where the flowers ever bloom, and the leaves ever shine?"

GENERAL DESCRIPTION

OF THE GRAND ORIENTAL BAZAAR

"CONSTANTINOPLE IN KENDAL."

THE Decorations will be on a magnificent scale, and are in the hands of our worthy townsman, Mr. ISAAC A. ROBINSON, who has engaged for that purpose Mr. GEO. M. BRIDGES of King's Lynn, Norfolk (Scenic Artist to H.R.H. the Prince of Wales) who will transform the interior of St. George's Hall so as to represent in a most realistic manner the beautiful "Crescent City of the Faithful."

This Bazaar is one of the latest productions of our celebrated Bazaar Artist, and on entering, the visitor will find himself in a Grand Square surrounded by some of the celebrated Bazaars and Markets of Constantinople. On all sides are Grand Palaces, Picturesque Mosques, Seraglios, Minarets, Towers, Fountains, and varied Latticed Windows, with rich traceries, Kiosks, Cupolas, and Domes, the exquisite carvings on which will doubtless attract attention. The whole of the scenery has been prepared from original sketches taken on the spot, displaying the beautiful Arabesque workmanship of the various edifices.

Pages from the brochure of the Grand Oriental Bazaar with elaborate illustrations and descriptions of the marvels to be found there.

improvements proposed were one new classroom for infants and two for older children, a technical instruction room for boys' woodwork and girls' cookery, and new cloakrooms and lavatories.

The cost of producing the brochure was defrayed by advertisements such as that by Braithwaite Bros. of Highgate picturing a sturdy lady's safety bicycle, guaranteed for 12 months and including free tuition for purchasers. Advertisements were also placed by various businesses owned by residents of Kendal Green at that time or at a later date including Bailie and Hargreaves, general and furnishing ironmongers of Central Buildings, Finkle Street, William Dinsdale, boot and shoe maker, 31/2 Finkle Street and James Wharton & Son, colliery agents, coal and coke merchants, 18 Market Place.

Only fifteen years later the school was almost totally destroyed by a fire that broke out on 1st December 1910. Again an appeal was made and a 'Grand International Bazaar' held to raise funds while the work of the school continued in three classrooms untouched by the fire and in rooms owned by the Wesleyan Church and the Fellside Sunday School. The Trustees listed in the appeal brochure included Isaac Braithwaite, Charles Butterwith of *Denmark House* (53 KG) and Miss Whitwell of 1 *Fairfield* (30 KG).

The architect for the rebuilt school was John Hutton of 22 Highgate who is known locally for houses he designed in Belmont and Burneside and Sedbergh roads as well as the Parish Hall, Kirkland.[4] The opportunity was taken to improve the school by the inclusion of a wide corridor running the length of the main building with light and spacious classrooms off to each side. Three separate blocks containing toilet and cloakroom were included within the walls of the main building 'a great step forward for those days, when toilets were usually small, rather primitive structures across the playground' (which some of the older readers of this history may well recall!).[5]

Late in 1925 the infant department was amalgamated into the so-called 'mixed department' of the School, i.e. for the older pupils. Then three years later the school was converted into Kendal Senior Girls' School and the infants section made independent again, but sharing the building with the senior girls. This was a consequence of the transfer elsewhere of other pupils as part of a re-organisation of all non-grammar schools in Kendal. In 1934 the infants' department was closed down finally; most pupils transferred to St. Thomas' School just down the road while the rest were sent to the town's other primary schools.

A few children from the locality went to Airethwaite School held in

1 Airethwaite, run by two sisters, Isabella and Elizabeth Nicholson who bought the house in 1888. In the 1881 Census they are shown as living with their brother just round the corner at 3 Albert Road East (63 KG).

At the school's prize giving ceremony held in December 1898 students named Ruth Pennington, Majorie Illingworth and Eric Nicholson were awarded prizes. These were probably the children of those named in censuses as living, respectively, at 2 *Fairbank* in 1901; 3 *Beechwood* in 1891; and 5 *Beechwood* in 1901. Ruth was awarded prizes for Class II overall and needlework, and was commended for 'regular attendance and punctuality', Marjorie was similarly commended as well as gaining the Class II prize for drawing and Eric was awarded the prize for music.

Also pupils at the school in 1891 were children of the Gawith family, Samuel and Connie, and among those on the rolls in 1898 were two of the children – Hubert and Hilda – of Arthur Simpson the carver and furniture designer. Both families were members of the Society of Friends.

The building of Underley houses from 1913 to 1928, then Hallgarth in the valley beyond after the Second World War and the houses on Empsom Road in the 1960s must have placed considerable pressure on the facilities offered by Kendal Green Girls' School. Within the town more generally the

Hutton's sketch of how the finished building would look.

raising of the school leaving age in 1947 and the predicted effects of children born in the post-war 'baby boom' reaching school age led the council to plan secondary modern schools. After much controversy caused by the Government's threat to renege on its commitment to contribute half towards the capital cost of the proposed school buildings, new boys' and girls' schools were built in the late 1950s on the Showfield site at Longlands. When Longlands Senior Girls' School was opened on 30th October 1958 it took in the pupils from Kendal Green School. From that date the building ceased to house a day school but continued in use for many years as accommodation for departments of the County Council. The Magistrates' Court was also held there during the period between the closure of the old court in the Town Hall and the opening in 1992 of the new one in Burneside Road.

THE MALTKILN AND CARPET FACTORY

After 1861 the maltkiln on Caroline Street, on the opposite side to the School, was subject to many changes of ownership and use. On the death of the original owner, Christopher Robinson, in the early 1830s his son-in-law, Henry Cragg, continued to run it until 1884 when Joseph Wiper

A drawing of the maltkiln after its conversion to a shop and dwelling house

bought the kiln for use as a factory. There Wiper experimented with the manufacture of mint cake. It is said that he often treated local young children to a handful of broken mint cake or other sweets manufactured there. In 1902 Wiper acquired a plot of land behind the maltkiln on which he built a fine house; its name, *Ferndene*, reflects his great interest in ferns, a wide variety of which still flourish in the garden.

Only ten years later, however, Wiper sold the maltkiln to the snuff and tobacco firm J.T. Illingworth & Sons. The machinery they installed was powered by town gas and continued in service until 1920 when Mr Wharton, a coal merchant and haulage contractor, bought the maltkiln for use as a furniture store.

In the second World War the authorities commandeered the kiln as an emergency food store but it was almost derelict by 1967 when bought by Richard Phillips to house the antique business he had built up at his shop in Wildman Street. He and his wife, Victoria, lived in the maltkiln after its renovation, moving there in 1968 from *Denmark House*, Kendal Green where they had lived since 1960.[6]

By 1868 carpets were being made nearby at the Factory at the bottom of the Green, owned previously by Gandy. An advert placed on 4th April that year in the *Kendal Mercury and Northern Advertiser*, and repeated over several weeks, announced that Martin and George Brown had started a 'carpet manufactory' there and were open for business.

HOUSE OF CORRECTION

The status of the House of Correction changed in 1888 when it became the county gaol and was called Kendal Prison, following the closure of the prison at Appleby. It was itself threatened with closure in 1893 but was reprieved upon ceasing to be a civilian gaol in 1894 when, for a few years, it became a military prison. It did not survive for long in the next century, however, and was sold at auction on 17th June 1907 by Messrs. M. De Rome and Son, referred to later in relation to Kendal Green. The bidding was started at £500 by a Mr Nelson – who may well have been the architect and builder who lived at *Holmfield* – but the prison buildings were eventually 'knocked down' to Mr Robert Pennington, builder for £1,000.

Pennington spent about 22 years demolishing the buildings while selling off the stone for use elsewhere in Kendal. It is claimed that some of this stone was used to build houses in Serpentine Road and other local roads.

KENDAL PRISON.

SALE BY AUCTION,

By Messrs. M. De Rome & Son,

AT THE TOWN HALL, KENDAL,

ON MONDAY, THE 17th DAY OF JUNE, 1907,

At 7 o'Clock in the Evening.

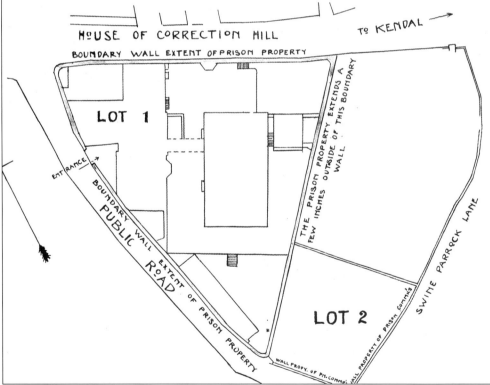

Page from the brochure advertising the sale of the Prison

Given the closeness of the prison site it is likely that the stone was also used in some of the houses built on Kendal Green in the 1920s and 1930s.

Looking up House of Correction Hill where, still looming over Town View, the main Prison block can be seen part demolished.

THE WORKHOUSE

Two important events in 1948 changed radically the role of the Workhouse. The National Assistance Act of that year placed on local authorities the duty of providing homes and other welfare services for elderly and handicapped people. In the same year the creation of the Health Service required more sick beds in State hospitals. So Kendal Green Workhouse was converted to fulfil a dual role: the provision of residential accommodation for the elderly and, in another part of the building, a hospital for elderly people who were sick. However, the stigma of 'Workhouse' remained and local old people are said to have been very reluctant to become residents or in-patients.

There was still the problem of 'vagrants', by then called 'wayfarers'. They continued to be accommodated in the nearby vagrants' ward where they were given a bed with clean sheets and a blanket for the night. Soup with bread and cheese was doled out to them at the hospital's kitchen door.

This situation lasted ten years until 1958 when the Local Authority moved those needing residential care out to other accommodation so that the old Workhouse buildings could be converted yet again, this time for sole use as a hospital for the elderly. Freda Exley was appointed matron in the following year, early enough to improve the plans for upgrading the building to allow, for example, more space around beds and, more surprising perhaps, for central heating. Extra staff were appointed including occupational therapists and other specialists who could assist patients' rehabilitation after illness or accident. Eventually, with the appointment of a Consultant in Geriatrics, full medical care could be provided in the hospital.

Kendal Green Hospital was closed following the opening of the Westmorland General in 1991. Then, despite objections from Caroline Street residents, planning permission was given in 1994 for the buildings to be converted by New Brunswick Properties for use as housing. A show house was opened during the following year.

A photograph of the housing development created from the Workhouse buildings along Caroline Street

CHAPTER IV

'THE GREEN' ITSELF

WHILE THE HOUSES may be of interest to some visitors to the Green most come for *The Green* itself – for the splendid grass area on which to play or relax, the beautiful trees and the relative tranquillity it provides in a busy town. From its acres they can also enjoy vistas to the north towards Whinfell round to the peaks above Kentmere, to the west up to the golf course on the Heights, to the south over the town and down the Kent Valley including the Helm and to the east across to Benson Knott.

CONSERVING, NAMING AND IMPROVING THE GREEN

The continued pleasure that people get from the Green derives in large part from the provisions of the two early Acts of Parliament relating to the land, which emphasised its use for the benefit of the ordinary folk of Kendal, and the way in which the Kendal Fell Trustees discharged their duties as defined in that legislation. Especially important was how they balanced their responsibilities for extending the use made of the Fell lands with those that obliged them to make provision for recreation, applying the bye-laws which they themselves had adopted in 1863.

Consistent with that obligation, the land between the two roads shown as Albert Road East and West on the 1862 map of plots to be sold around Low Tenter Fell was labelled 'Recreation Ground'. Perhaps it is also significant that in response to a petition in 1870 from owners and occupiers the Trustees agreed to lay out walks and plant trees, but they did not seem to have acceded to the request that they should 'rail in the Green' although gates were erected to regulate access.

The matter of the status of the Green was settled finally on 6th February 1970 when it was registered formally as a 'Town Green' under the provisions of the Commons Registration Act of 1965. A key document on this issue was the 1907 Kendal Corporation Act, under which the powers of the Kendal Fell Trust were transferred to Kendal Corporation. In a Schedule attached to the Act key provisions of the 1767 and 1861 Acts relating to Kendal Fell were reaffirmed and other commitments taken. In Part II of the Schedule two parcels of land are described, referred to earlier, which were 'set apart and appropriated for the use of the inhabitants of Kendal for recreation ground...'. The first is Bowling Fell and the second Kendal Green, is defined as 'six acres of land on the north side of and adjoining to the road from the House of Correction Hill to Greenbank' (i.e. Green Road and Horncop Lane) and bounded on the east by gardens belonging to the said township lands and on the north and west by said township lands' (where township lands refers to those which are part of Kendal Fell).

As for the name 'Kendal Green', when one considers the greenness of the area the reason seems fairly obvious especially in a town famous for its green cloth. This is the 'Kendal Green' referred to by Shakespeare in *Henry IV, part one* when Falstaff tells of 'three misbegotten knaves in Kendal-Green' who he alleges attacked him on a pitch black night! We can be fairly certain, for example, that this usage inspired the naming of the *Kendal Green* public house on House of Correction Hill referred to earlier. But who decided to name this part of Kendal Fell so, and when?

The answer stems from a decision made early in 1864 to celebrate the three hundredth anniversary of Shakespeare's birthday, 23rd April 1564. The day set aside for the event was Monday 25th April when it was arranged that Kendal's school children should be granted a half-day holiday and tradesmen would be asked to close their shops at an early hour in the afternoon.

The *Kendal Mercury and Northern Advertiser* reported, in the following Saturday's edition, that on the day when the celebration was held in Kendal similar events were held around England: in Stratford-on-Avon, London – where a working men's demonstration took place in the city and an oak was planted on Primrose Hill – in Penrith, Carlisle and Wigton. Even the Archbishop of Dublin preached at St James, praising Shakespeare as a great gift from God.

At one-o-clock in the afternoon of 25th April the Kendal bells started ringing and an hour later there was a large body of children in the Market Place accompanied by the Rifle Band, Mr Wallace's Band and the

Workhouse Union Drum and Fife band, all marshalled and directed by the Mayor.

In the words of the *Mercury's* reporter,

> ...*about 1,500 children had been assembled and proceeded, with a band of music in front and another in the rear, to the Tenter Fell. The children also carried a large number of flags and banners kindly supplied by Mr Foster Braithwaite whose exertions throughout for the success of the celebration has been beyond any praise of ours. The procession was now directed towards the Low Tenter Fell where a large number of people – we have heard the number on the Fell, young and old estimated at 5,000 – soon assembled to witness the planting of the Shakespeare Oak.*
>
> *At the sound of the bugle there was silence and the Mayor, in a few remarks, explained the object of planting an oak to the memory of England's greatest poet. He then introduced to the people Master John Wakefield a child of about six years of age who went to work vigorously to dig the hole and plant the tree and name it 'Shakespeare's Oak', after which the Mayor hoisted the young gentleman on his shoulders and presented him to the people amid loud cheers as the workman of the day.*
>
> *Mr Whitwell also, in a few words, referred to the connection of Mr Wakefield and Mr W.H. Wakefield to Kendal and trusted that Master Wakefield, whose first public act had been performed today, would follow in the footsteps of his father and grandfather and prove a blessing to those around him in future days.*
>
> *The Mayor then, hoisting aloft a large green placard bearing the words 'Kendal Green', said that he had great pleasure in naming the plot of ground on which they were now assembled Kendal Green, by which name it would, henceforth, be known. It was a part of the ground secured for the public for everlasting possession and it was fitly baptised by this name today, for no one had done so much to wed the two names, 'Kendal' and 'Green', together...'.*

After the ceremony,

> ...'*the children were marched through a tent, which the Mayor had placed on the ground, and each was presented with a medal and ribbon complete for wearing and a bun, to the number of 1,200 medals and 1,500 buns. And as the children passed out, at the other end of the tent a good-natured townsman, Mr Greenwood, grocer,*

presented each with a packet of lozenges, and then when they were
fairly out they were met with a very welcome scramble of nuts etc.
by Mr W.H. Wakefield.

… we are certain the pleasant faces and smiles of the young was
a reward sufficient to the gentlemen who so energetically collected
the funds and to those who generously supplied them.

The tree was broken down the same day – we trust accidentally
– but it is now restored and railed in. It will flourish we trust for
very many generations and the great-great grandchildren of the
least children present at the celebration will sit for shelter in their
old age beneath the broad branches of 'Shakespeare's Oak on Kendal
Green'.

In the evening 'a Shakespearean literary and musical entertainment' was
held in the Albert Buildings. It had been planned as 'a good old-fashioned
social tea where ladies could enjoy themselves as well as gentlemen, seated
at tables and not standing after the new style', for an entrance fee of 1s-6d.
Those who attended were given an introductory address, a eulogy to

The tree that is believed to be the Shakespeare Oak during its 135th winter on the Green.

Shakespeare and the English language and were then entertained by instrumentalists Messrs. Braithwaite, Armstrong, Hogg and Gibson, the Rifle Band under its bandmaster, Mr James Smith, and vocal performances.

The only oak tree currently growing which could date from that time and located where the planting is said to have taken place – 'in the centre of the west side' – is opposite *Silver Howe* and *Overdale* (23 & 24 KG). In his note about this event, Curwen also recommends that there 'is the need of some tablet to record its history'.[1] Perhaps a hundred years after he wrote this we could arrange to do what he suggests?

The reference to this special tree reminds us of the many fine trees on the Green, at least some of which may have been planted at about the same time as the Shakespeare Oak. Yet on the first edition OS map based on an 1858 survey no trees are shown on the land used as a recreation area, despite the fact that the trees in the triangular copse to the west mentioned earlier are shown in some detail. Curwen is helpful in explaining how some of the trees come to be there in his reference to three fir trees planted to commemorate the marriage of the Prince of Wales. But that fact makes more sense when related to another event, on 10th March 1863, when the then Mayor of Kendal, Councillor J. Whitwell, planted two Wellingtonia in Serpentine Woods to commemorate the marriage of the Prince of Wales (later King Edward VII) to Princess Alexandra of Denmark.[2] So

Wellingtonia photographed from the west side of the Green near the Shakespeare Oak

it is quite likely that the two magnificent Wellingtonia that still stand on the Green are two of the three 'fir trees' Curwen refers to and were also planted to commemorate the marriage.

Certainly the fact that Alexandra was a Princess of Denmark is thought to explain why 53 Kendal Green – near where the Wellingtonias stand – is called *Denmark House* and why the first terrace of three houses built on the Green as early as 1864 was called *Denmark Terrace.*

Curwen also notes that 'in April 1870, other trees were added on three sides of the Green', a very cryptic acknowledgement of the work of the Kendal Fell Trustees in planting trees and maintaining them despite regular vandalism. Evidence of their efforts in this regard is littered throughout the minutes of their meetings from 1870 until at least 1902.

Some who lived near the Green in the 1940s remember more large trees around its verges then, including a massive beech tree at the junction with Underley Road and two very big sweet chestnut trees and one horse chestnut, the focus of much collecting of nuts in season. Under the trees, plants grew called 'pignuts', a member of the carrot family, which children grubbed up and ate their tuber-like roots.

Marjorie Crossley recalls how, when she first lived here in the 1920s, few trees grew on the body of the Green; a copse on the north side of the tenter hill was very sparse. By the time Eileen Russell came to live at *Empson Hill* in 1964 there was a well established plantation, mainly larches, in that position and only later were trees planted on the terraced slope to the south. Unfortunately this planting eventually obscured the tenter terracing as happened at about the same time on Prickley Fell. The trees also hide a shallow rectangular depression – about four yards wide and ten long, surrounded by concrete slabs – which, certainly in the 1950s, served as a sandpit for local children. Finally, at the north end of the existing woodland, twelve trees, including an aspen, were planted in 1986 to commemorate the expansion of the European Union to that number of members consequent on the accession of Spain and Portugal.

RECREATION GROUND

Since the time the Green was first designated in law as a recreation ground it will have been used in many different ways over the intervening years. The part most favoured has probably always been the flat area to the south used for organised football and cricket and, beyond that, near the old factory where bonfires were lit until quite recently.

There is evidence that it was used in the late 18th century by prison inmates as recorded in a story, perhaps apocryphal, concerning a prison keeper by the name of Miles Hayton, or 'Miley Honey'. He is said to have taken prisoners out for exercise and to play football on Low Tenter Fell. Then, when it was time for them to return he would shout, 'Noo lads, you mun follow me, or if you don't, I'll lock you oot'.[3]

The preservation of the Green as a recreation ground was part of the Trustees' role. In April 1862 they were instructing the surveyor to arrange for the recreation ground to be levelled. Much later still they were responding to requests for grass seed to improve the cricket ground and to ensure that the football posts were removed but one year they were still up in July. As late as 1909, after the Trust had been incorporated into the Council, a plan was approved for a major project to lift the flat part of the lower end of the Green by several inches.

As now, families who lived nearby have probably played on parts of the Green for the whole of the period since the time when the prisoners exercised, although for many years after the 1767 Act tenter frames would have restricted its recreational use. Organised games have also been arranged by local schools which did not have their own playing fields, and by adult soccer teams.

Pupils of Kendal Green school played games on the Green until the school was closed in 1958 and the girls of Holly Croft School probably played there too during its brief life. Jim Richardson, who lived for some time at 5 Green Road, remembers being given cricket coaching on the Green by a Mr Robertson who told him to 'give it a good slog'. So he did and hit the ball so hard that it soared over Albert Road East and crashed into the timber upright of one of the bay windows. Jim was greatly relieved that no glass was broken because he doubted that his widowed mother could have afforded to pay for the damage.[4]

In 1921 a soccer club based at Kendal Green joined the Westmorland County Football Association. In the following year two of the twenty teams competing for the 'Hospital Cup' were *Kendal Green Villa* and *Kendal Green Athletic*.[5] Colin Martindale tells how in 1944 when older players were returning from military service and younger ones awaited call-up for National Service, those who lived locally – in Burneside Road, Cross Street, Union Street, Underley etc. – formed a team which they called *Kendal Green Rovers*. But the Green, which had no goal-posts then, was used only for training sessions; matches were played on the Jubilee playing fields. Colin became Secretary of the club when he returned from military service in 1950. At that date there was a ban on 'official' Sunday matches so the *Rovers* played in a Sunday 'friendly' league.

At first the team wore naval ratings' shirts, white short-sleeved with square neck edged in blue. Then funds were raised locally to buy a proper 'strip' including shirts of green and white squares. They designed their own badge and a neighbour's daughter embroidered them and sewed them onto the thirteen shirts.

Someone else who remembers the *Rovers* is Jack Williams who was involved with the team from about 1966; he contributed the photograph shown below. Jack understands that football posts were used on the Green at some earlier time, taken down after every game as still happens at clubs such as Staveley. The *Rovers* stopped playing at the Jubilee grounds in 1977 to move to Endmoor but, to commemorate their roots on the Green, they took the name *Endmoor KGR*. Teams from the club still play in the Talbot Insurance Westmorland League and in 2002 the club celebrated 25 years at Endmoor.

Earlier on local children were much less constrained than now in what they could do and in their freedom to roam freely and relatively safely beyond the Green. Even as late as the early 1950s they could follow the rocky path to the east leading steeply down immediately north of *Highfield*

Photograph of Kendal Green Rovers team in 1946–47 season taken in the Labour Hall in Blackhall Yard where the club held fund-raising events.

(*50 KG*) into the valley beyond, then up the other side to Prickley Fell and over to Horncop along the path that still rises out of the Empsom Road estate. Similarly, to the west it was still possible to venture quite freely across Windermere Road and up to the 'Heights', Kendal common land and golf course.

When there was snow on the ground early in the 20th century sledges could be ridden with impunity down Smith's Hill (called that after a Mr Smith who lived at *10 Beechwood* despite its formal name, Green Hill) and on over the banks of the Green itself. Even much later in the century it was possible to sledge down the track that became Empsom Road and, for the 'whitest knuckle' ride, down the very steep slope into Hallgarth.

ROADS AND MODERN VEHICLES

The Fell Trustees' minutes chronicle the beginning of the road making era that eventually allowed the burgeoning of motorised traffic around and across the Green. As early as a meeting on Christmas Eve 1861 the Trustees received a report from their surveyor that the 'Guardians' (of the Workhouse) had selected 'the most able bodied men… to make the road on Low Tenter Fell'. In 1864 the surveyor was submitting plans of Albert Roads East and West for the Trustees' agreement and three years later was instructed to 'metal Albert Road East'. The construction of a road leading from Ambleside Road (now Windermere Road) to Kendal Green was agreed in 1870 and in the same year the surveyor's estimate was accepted for 'erecting new gate stoops and a new gate at the entrance to Kendal Green'. Then in December 1872 the Trustees sanctioned a road to be made 'across Kendal Green from Fairfield towards *Denmark House*, that Albert Road East be re-formed and repaired, that a new gateway and gate be erected at the end of Albert Road West opposite the Factory and that additional trees be planted on the Green'.

Other minor work was done involving, for example, the removal in April 1862 of a pinfold (an enclosure in which stray sheep were kept until their owners reclaimed them) from the corner opposite the old factory and its re-erection elsewhere. The pinfold is marked quite clearly in its original position on the 1858 OS map.

The gates were still in operation in the 1920s, serving to close off the Green completely, joined as they were to each end of the straight wall that still runs east to west between Green Road and Horncop Lane south of the Green. It seems that the gates remained in use until some of the residents

This photograph shows the position of the gate at the south-east corner of Kendal Green with the stoops still in position

of *Wood Lea* and *Beechwood* terraces complained to the Council at having to pay an annual fee of one shilling and eleven pence for the privilege of gaining access to their houses while the residents of the newly created Underley Estate to the north-west of the Green could walk through without payment.

Eventually the gates were removed and the western end of the wall was extended in a curve along the first part of Albert Road West to stop people immediately turning to walk across the grass as they entered the Green from the direction of town. Some twenty years later the local roads were renamed, surprisingly during the Second World War. The Borough Council decided on 20th February 1941 to change to 'Kendal Green' the names of the roads that ran around the Green itself, and into the extension to the north-east, and to number the houses sequentially from 1 (i.e. *1 Wood Lea*) to 65 (*1 Albert Road East*).[6]

At that time and for years later the Green was better served by shops than it is now. A Post Office remained open until the 1990s just in Windermere Road around the corner from the newsagents and general store that, fortunately, still remains open today.

On Windermere Road to the north of Green Road, just behind *Wood Lea* terrace, was another general store and at the north-western corner of

Early 20th century photograph of Green Road and the corner shop run for many years by Helen Hall.

Members of Kendal Cycle Club line up for a photograph before riding off.

the Green a very busy shop, called Tysons, was sited on Fairfield Lane where there is now a television and video repair workshop.

By the time the gates were removed from the two Albert roads, modern vehicles had long been in use in Kendal and on the roads around the Green. Cycles were quite common in the town as early as the late 1870s, and in 1896 a cycle warehouse was opened in Wildman Street in response to what Bingham describes as a 'bicycle mania'. Four year's later, as part of a fete to raise funds for Kendal's Home Nursing Association, twenty young ladies, 'dressed in white costumes and white straw hats', took part in 'a bicycle gymkhana' during which they completed 'a twelve-minute musical ride which included two miles of maze threading and other intricate manoeuvres'.[7]

Such events were clearly still in fashion in 1909 when Mrs Fildes invited a group of women to tea in the garden of *Overdale (24KG)* before they went to a cycle parade in the evening. The diaries of her friend, Margaret Shaw, also tell of cycle rides when the two of them went to Underbarrow and Bowness.

Charles Fildes obtained planning permission in 1904 for Martindales to build a 'cycle house' in which he almost certainly kept two tricycles he owned, one of which was motorised. Apart from Fildes, others who lived on the Green are known to have been keen motor cyclists, including James Ruthven, a commercial traveller, who had a 'cycle store' built in 1914 at his home, *6 Wood Lea,* a younger man, Hugh Livingstone, whose family also lived in the same terrace and the Harrison brothers – Rupert from *Overdale* and Hal from *Highfield.* Both James Ruthven and Hugh Livingstone were killed in accidents when riding their motor-cycles.

The Harrisons also owned cars as did other local people, including David Dodds of *Oakdene* and Eric Nicholson at *5 Beechwood.* The growth of car ownership is reflected in planning applications for eleven garages at houses on Kendal Green between 1911 and 1932.

Despite this trend, car ownership was still quite rare so that cars were probably an even more important mark of status among men then than they are now. This may explain rivalry between the Harrison brothers as when Rupert complained that his brother, Hal's, Ford V8 was 'large, flashy and tinny'. The two also competed in hill climbs at which Rupert drove a Morgan whereas, at some point, Hal drove an Alfa Romeo. David Dodds, of *Oakdene,* and his son George who lived next door at the *Newlands,* were also keen motorists as was John Dyson, the architect who built his own

Charles Fildes on his motor-tricycle in the lane at the back of Overdale between Kendal Green and Windermere Road. According to records held in the Cumbria Records Office in Kendal, the vehicle was a Coventry Notette, registered as EC 152 in 1904, the year in which Fildes was seventy.

David Dodds at the wheel of his tourer at the beginning of a family holiday in Scotland with his wife Mary and son, George, seen here peering out from the back seat.

George Dodds standing by his Chrysler in 1938, parked in the back lane behind Oakdene. His father, David, is on the far side.

Ist May 1900: after an ascent of House of Correction Hill competitors in the Automobile Club's 1,000 mile trial give their cars a breather at the corner of Green Road.[8]

house at 44 Kendal Green. He is remembered as the owner of an Armstrong Siddeley Tourer which he drove wearing trilby and sun-glasses.

At that time the Westmorland Motor Club, formed in January 1910, was very active; the Harrison brothers were members as was George Dodds who was Treasurer of the club during part of his thirty years as a member.

Until the 1960s it seems that motor vehicles were allowed to be driven along the two paths which cross Kendal Green. Presumably, when the decision was made to ban cars from these paths, the tubular steel barriers were erected to allow only pedestrians to pass through.

On 23rd July 1962 the grass itself was used by a much less conventional vehicle as recounted by Michael Crossley then home on vacation at 10 Kendal Green. Very early one morning his mother woke him, rushing into his bedroom in great excitement to tell him to come quickly; there were people out on the Green and someone had laid out a large 'H' not far from their house.

Immediately, Michael got dressed, grabbed his camera and went out into the bright early sun-light. He soon gleaned that a glider had crashed and a decision had been taken to bring the crew by helicopter to Kendal.

Helicopter on the Green early morning with ambulance in attendance.

By the time the helicopter landed at about 7 am an ambulance was wait-
ing to take the injured pilot to hospital.

It seems that two members of the Lakes Gliding Club had taken off the
previous evening from the club's airfield near Tebay and had soon become
engulfed in mist and cloud. Without suitable instruments for 'flying blind'
and despite the pilot's efforts to turn the glider away from the higher
ground it crashed on the Howgill fells above Tebay. The pilot was injured
but able to hobble to the nearest farm and thence to a telephone. Early the
next morning sheets from Westmorland County Hospital, where the
patients were to be taken for treatment, were used to lay out an 'H' to
guide the helicopter onto the Green.

QUARRY AND PIGGERY

Relationships with the Guardians of the Workhouse featured regularly in
the minutes of the Trust, concerning not only the use made of paupers for
building roads but also, in a connected enterprise, the management of a
quarry at the north end of the Green. This stemmed from a provision of
the 1861 Act which gave the Trust the power to lease to any person for a
period of not more than 21 years parts of the township lands for establishing quarries and to 'dig for, take, and carry away such stone as shall be
found therein, together with full liberty to set up lime-kilns on such
lands…'.[9] The first Trust minute that relates to Kendal Green on this issue
refers to an agreement of 1880 that the Guardians of Kendal Union should
be able to supply stone from the quarry on payment to the Trust of £12 per
house supplied. By 1889 the Trust's income from this source was about £17
a year.

In 1884, as a result of a report made by a trustee, Matthew De Rome,
on how the quarry was being worked, it was agreed that it must not be
worked to a depth of more than ten feet in order that thereafter the land
might be made available for building. Three years later De Rome complained about stones – referred to as 'blue seth' – piled at the corner of the
road leading from the Green to 'Ambleside Road'. A subcommittee of the
Trustees was then set up to meet with the Guardians to agree some place
on which stones from the quarry could be deposited.

Despite the concern shown in 1884 about the eventual restoration of
the quarry site for development, four years later the Trustees allowed the
Guardians to take more ground for use as a quarry provided that they
arranged for the repair of damage done by quarry operations to Kendal

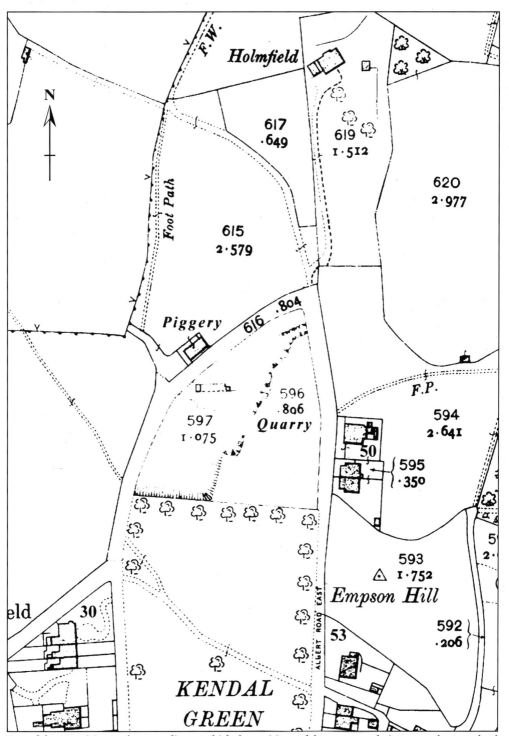

Part of the 1911 OS map shown earlier on which the positions of the quarry and piggery can be seen clearly.

Green Roads. When the Guardians tried to persuade the Trust to employ 'the steam roller to put Albert Road East and West in proper condition for some years' using materials provided from the quarry, they were given short shrift and told to carry out the repairs without the use of the steamroller. Despite this extension of the area given over to quarrying, in the following year the Trust was considering the 'question of whether the Kendal Green quarry should be filled up again for the purpose of Garden Ground or building sites' and, in a separate minute, was asking the 'quarry committee and surveyor to arrange for a basic mode of clearing up the quarry'. Yet again, almost eighteen months afterwards, the surveyor was being instructed by the Trustees 'to draw attention of the Kendal Union to the fact that they were working the quarry on Kendal Green about two feet below the level as stipulated in the agreement'.

In the back garden of 46 Kendal Green, on the very steep slope north of Empsom Road, a cache of discarded clay smoking pipes was found. A local historian suggested that this may have been where quarry workers had a hut. In this case, they may have worked in a quarry on the Green or one that was cut into the sharp edge to the east, in or near the garden.

The position of the quarry in the north-west corner of the Green is clearly marked on the 1911 OS map as can be seen on the previous page.

In her reminiscences of living in Kendal, Rita Groat, born there in 1910, refers to a 'group of paupers from the poor house', who she saw sitting at the top of Kendal Green breaking up stone.[10] Others have told recently how they saw paupers at work after 1920 splitting stones while sitting on the road beyond the wall on the southern boundary of the Green and working at a quarry at the north end. Another report suggests that the quarry had not been filled in as late as 1929 when, every day, two old men wheeled a barrow up from the Workhouse carrying rubbish for dumping in the quarry and edible material to feed the pigs in the neighbouring piggery.

Again the 1911 OS map is helpful, this time in showing where the piggery stood just north of Albert Road West in the south-west corner of what is now St. Thomas' school playing field. It was probably erected on that site at the north end of the Green after a complaint in 1898 from the town's Health Committee. This may have been initiated by residents of Ferney Green about a nuisance caused by pigs kept near to the 'Vagrant Ward' which maps show was sited near Ferney Green. In response the Trust put in hand the building of a new piggery 'on old quarry ground on the north-east side of the Green'.

Much later a planning application for piggeries on Kendal Green for

Kendal Union was agreed in 1907 to a design by 'William Levens, architect', perhaps the same person who, with Martin Hodgson, was involved in the development of much housing on the Green.

The piggery and nearby vegetable plots, part of which was given over to a 'potato ground', were administered by the Guardians of the Workhouse, providing work for the paupers and, presumably, food and income to help in maintaining the buildings and facilities. The piggery still existed in the 1940s but the quarry had been filled in, leaving a quite scrubby area rather than a well tended field. In the early 1960s the piggery was demolished in preparation for the building of the new school.

VANDALISM AND 'PUBLIC NUISANCES'

Complaints about public nuisance of one sort or another committed on the Green were submitted regularly to the Trust, often concerning the bad behaviour of young people. Frequently they were accused of vandalising trees; in 1899, for example, damage done to two trees by 'two boys called Wilson from Caroline Street' (shock-horror!) was serious enough to warrant their being called before the Trustees so that the Chairman could elicit a promise of 'good behaviour' from them. Presumably, in this situation the Trustees could have applied the clause written into their bye-laws allowing them to impose on the culprit 'a penalty for each offence of any sum not exceeding two pounds'.

On other occasions, it seems, the nuisance was an even greater threat to public order as when in June 1889 the Trustees considered a long letter from Theodore DeRome on behalf of the 'Kendal Green Protection Association'. Several complaints were made about 'rude and unruly youths' including a claim that they were seen 'completely undressing themselves and putting on football costume in broad daylight on the Green (7.40 PM Tuesday 7th June) to the annoyance and disgust of several ladies who were in their gardens adjoining the Green'. The letter went on that 'Thomas Hill and George Rigg of Denmark Road are prepared to come forward as witnesses'. It was suggested that a meeting of the Trust's committee for Kendal Green and the residents 'would help to restore order'!

We have no idea whether members of the Kendal Fell Trust gained much satisfaction from dealing with such incidents. However, given the relentless stream of similarly trivial issues raised not only by Kendal Green residents but also those owning property on other parts of the Fell lands, the Trustees could surely have been forgiven a sigh of relief when their duties were taken over in 1907 by Kendal Corporation. Even as late as 1930, though, it was still seen as necessary to have a special Committee of the Town Council – made up of two aldermen and three councillors – to deal with the affairs of Kendal Green. As noted already in relation to the 'recreation ground' aspect of the Green and the care of its trees, the local council still fulfils this role.

CHAPTER V

THE SHAKERS AND SHAPERS

Now WE TURN our attention to those who were influential in shaking up the previous political and social order and shaping a new environment and community around Low Tenter Fell. This continues the thread of the previous chapter in that the Kendal Fell Trustees were probably the key group over a long period. For many years before building was started on the Green they were active in drumming up support, both personal and financial, for the task of getting legislation put before Parliament passed eventually as the 1861 Act which allowed development on Fell lands. Once plots of land were offered for sale by the Trust other groups became influential: the developers, architects and builders. Then as houses were built and occupied the Trustees assumed the role of administrators of what were, in effect, estates of private houses. The minutes of their meetings suggest that – despite the criticism referred to earlier that the Trust was not ideally suited for its role and, hence, did not perform it well – they took great pains over more than forty years to administer Kendal Green under the new dispensation, and to deal with a host of fresh problems it brought. As they quickly found out, there's nothing like property ownership to 'up the ante' in public affairs!

THE KENDAL FELL TRUSTEES

The Trustees in 1861 were the Mayor of Kendal together with James Bousefield, G. A. Gelderd, Thomas Harrison, John Hudson, J. G. J. Ireland, John Ireland, Samuel Rhodes, Thomas Simpson, William Wakefield, John Whitwell, John Jowitt Wilson and W. Wilson. The Superintendent of Lands was H. Hoggarth, Land Surveyor, Finkle Street.

The Quaker Families

Three long-standing and influential Quaker families were represented – the Wakefields, Whitwells and Wilsons – to be joined before long by members of the Braithwaite family of similar local standing. Long before 1861, however, most members of these families – as well as the Bensons, Crewdsons and Croppers – had left the Society of Friends as a result of deep divisions within its national membership between those who held to its tradition of 'inwardness' and 'Quietism' and others who were attracted to the more outward-looking evangelism of the other churches. As a result membership of the Kendal Meeting fell sharply through expulsions and resignations from the late 1830s on. Some who left turned to various evangelical churches, others to the Church of England.[1]

Apart from William Wakefield (1828–1899), who served from 1861 until at least 1875, his cousin, also William (1825–1893), was a Trustee for more than eight years from 1861. Initially each was listed in the Trust minutes as 'banker' but when re-elected that was transmuted into 'gentleman'. As noted already, both of them, together with George Foster Braithwaite, were signatories for the Trustees when Trust land was conveyanced in 1866 to George Rigg for the building of 4 Albert Road East.

John Whitwell was probably the best known of many prominent manufacturers who served as Trustees. He was Mayor of Kendal in 1861, ran a carpet and rug manufacturing company at Dockwray Hall Mills but still found time to act as mayor six times, to become a Liberal MP for Kendal and to support various charitable causes. J.G. Ireland, a Trustee from 1861, was also a rug manufacturer.

Trustees drawn from the very extensive Wilson family of Kendal were descendants on one side of Thomas Wilson, 1664–1719, and his son, William, 1677–1734, both tanners of Stramongate and, on the other side, Isaac Wilson 1714–1785, a shearman, dyer and drysalter and woollen dealer. Isaac was the youngest son of Anthony and Dorothy Wilson of High Wray and came to Kendal, probably in 1732, to be apprenticed to a Quaker firm of shearman dyers. In 1740 he married Rachel Wilson, granddaughter of Thomas Wilson via his daughter Deborah, the wife of John Wilson a tanner of Highgate.[2]

The Wilsons intermarried with the Braithwaites and the Wakefields, all very influential Kendal Quakers and businessmen. John Jowitt Wilson was a Trustee for at least seven years from 1861 while Isaac Whitwell Wilson became a Trustee in the later 1870s. John's period as a Trustee overlapped with that of his cousin Charles Lloyd Braithwaite appointed in 1864. John built and lived in *Underfell* on Greenside next door to *Ghyll Close* built by Charles as his family home.

Charles Lloyd Braithwaite and his younger brother, George Foster Braithwaite, were Trustees for a number of years, part of a Kendal business dynasty probably started by one of their Quaker ancestors, George Braithwaite, 1683–1735. The first family firm was set up to supply vegetable and chemical based dyes to Kendal's woollen industry from premises acquired in 1701 situated in an area behind Highgate, now known as Dr. Mannings Yard. George's son, also George, 1714–1753, was a dyer or shearman dyer and his son, again George, 1746–1812, lived in the Highgate house which straddled the yard. It was one of his sons, Isaac, 1781–1861, who gave his name to the firm, Isaac Braithwaite and Son, Drysalters.

Charles Lloyd and George Foster Braithwaite established a second family firm in 1837, Braithwaite and Co. They acquired Meal Bank Mill, about a mile upstream from Kendal on the River Mint, which they ran as a woollen and linsey mill. A turbine was installed there to replace the water

Braithwaite Yard, now Dr. Mannings Yard.

wheel in 1895, enabling the company to continue manufacturing linseys, tweeds and horse cloths well into the twentieth century. Another company to use the family name was founded by Isaac Braithwaite; he is referred to later regarding his ownership of houses on Kendal Green.[3]

Members of the Braithwaite, Wilson and Wakefield families had direct financial interests in the development of Kendal Green as revealed in the deeds of a mortgage taken out by George Rigg in 1866 and a later one by John Robinson in 1869. Both were with the Kendal and Northern Counties Permanent Benefit Building Society for which the signatories were William Wakefield, Isaac Whitwell Wilson and Charles Lloyd Braithwaite 'the younger'.

Samuel Gawith was Trustee from 1861 to his death in 1865, when he was serving as Mayor of Kendal. As a young man he had eloped with, and married at Gretna Green, a daughter of Thomas Harrison who ran a firm of tobacco and snuff manufacturers. On Harrison's death his partner, a Mr Brocklebank, took Samuel into partnership.[4]

Trustees local to Kendal Green

Only two householders from Kendal Green served as Trustees, Charles Butterwith, a grocer who lived at *Denmark House* until 1919 and joined the Trustees in 1900 and Joseph Jordan, the corn merchant of *Oakdene*, who became a Trustee in 1904 not long before the Council took over the Trust's role.

As noted in the last section, one Trustee, Matthew De Rome, who lived round the corner at *Airethwaite* took a special interest in Kendal Green, the same person who was summonsed in 1874 for owning unfit houses. (In early records the name was listed as Derome and it was only later that it began to appear as DeRome or De Rome). Apart from his earlier ad hoc involvement with the Green, Matthew De Rome was appointed in 1889 to a standing committee 'to superintend Kendal Green and the working of the quarry'. At that time he was principal of a firm of auctioneers and chartered accountants, *M. De Rome and Son*, with offices in Stramongate. His son, Theodore De Rome, who lived at *4 Beechwood Terrace (10 KG)*, was a member of the same firm described in the 1891 Census records as 'auctioneer, accountant, estate agent'. As noted already, he acted on behalf of the 'Kendal Green Protection Association' in dealing with the Trust.

In 1868 a De Rome had bought two of the plots of land on which the terrace of houses Nos. 56–59 KG was built in the 1920s. For people with these sorts of professional and private interests the building of high quality houses taking place on the Green would have been of considerable significance as would have been the fate of the quarry, the stone it produced and the eventual use made of the land on which it was worked.

DEVELOPERS, BUILDERS AND ARCHITECTS

When plots of land were available the shaping of the Green was taken up by three overlapping groups of people: would-be house owners and/or developers who bought the land and determined how it was to be used, qualified architects who, in a few cases, designed the houses or advised on their design and, of course, the builders who seem often to have doubled up as architects.

In this context the most influential group were those we would call nowadays 'developers'. The earliest and most important was Martin Hodgson, described in deeds as 'Foreman of Woollen Mill' and later 'Mill Manager'. He was involved in the purchase of land for, and construction of, 24 of the current total of 30 houses on the west side of the Green. The six houses of *Wood Lea* and ten of *Beechwood* were built on land acquired jointly by Hodgson and William Levens, a builder who designed the two terraces. He lived on Ferney Green where Hodgson was once a neighbour; then later they moved 'up market' and lived near each other at *Highfield Villas* now part of Windermere Road. At some stage they were also given planning permission to build the first two houses of the *Villas*. Nothing else is known about either of the partners.

In acquiring land and building two pairs of semi-detached houses just north of Green Hill (*1 and 2 Fairbank, Holly Bank and Laurel Mount*) Hodgson and Levens were joined by a Mr Wiper. It is possible he was Joseph Wiper who, as noted above, was a manufacturer of Kendal Mint Cake living at *Ferndene* just off Maltkiln Hill near Ferney Green.

Hodgson may have been stretched to finance his various building projects which could be inferred from his decision to sell *6 Wood Lea* to J.H. Ruthven on 12th November 1887 and to lease it back under an agreement of the same date. Moreover, of £590 realised by the sale only £190 went to Hodgson; the balance was due to Hoggarth, a mortgagee. The lease involved an annual rent of £30 and ran until Whit Wednesday, 1890.

Hodgson's last venture on the Green, with no partners noted in the deeds, was to buy the land and arrange for the building of the two pairs of semi-detached houses (23–26 KG) between *Oakdene* and *Fairfield Terrace*. Perhaps he was less assured on this occasion since he twice changed his mind about what exactly he intended to build and, even then, failed to complete the venture.

Hodgson died in 1917 leaving 24 Kendal Green to his son, Arthur Nicholas Whitfield Hodgson, an architect referred to below, and a William Dodd.

George Rigg was involved earlier than Hodgson as a developer/builder and architect of seven houses on Albert Road East. First he built *Nos. 1–3 Albert Road East* for John Birkett in 1864 and then bought land further up the road on which he built at least the right hand house of the pair of semi-detached houses, Nos. 4 and 5. He went on to build Nos. 6 and 7 after the plans were agreed in 1865 and, finally, No. 8, *Denmark House*. Rigg also built at least one house on Airethwaite as well as Kendal Green School, referred to earlier. Further afield, he is shown on planning applications for buildings in Wildman Street, a house on High Fellside, a Methodist Chapel in Blackhall and a warehouse and stable in Woolpack Yard.

Much later a local builder, William Dixon, was active on the Green; his company was involved in the construction of nine houses. Having acquired land sold originally to others in 1868 but left undeveloped he gained permission in 1922 to build the terrace of four houses now numbered 56–59 Kendal Green.

In the early 1930s Dixon's firm worked on the Green's north-east extension, building a pair of semi-detached houses, Nos. 42 and 43 on land administered by Nelson's executors. It is not known who designed these houses nor the bungalow, *The Whins*, Dixon built for a Mr Hoggarth on land owned by Dixon. However, he did use one of his own 'stock designs' for another pair of houses, Nos. 48 and 49, built on land he purchased himself.[5]

Only six qualified architects are known to have been involved in designing houses on the Green: Michael Bottomley, John Dyson, Arthur Hodgson, Alfred Nelson, Malcolm Shaw and Stephen Shaw. It is likely that Rigg and Levens, who were listed in planning applications as 'architects', had no formal training. This was possible for most of the period under consideration even though the Institute of British Architects had been granted its first royal charter in 1837 by William IV and had established a night school in London for architectural studies ten years later. Despite this, until 1931 membership continued to be open to individuals on the basis of recommendation by senior architects after a period of work as articled junior in a recognised practice. After 1931 architects were licensed to practise only after passing qualification tests administered by the Royal

Institute of British Architects (RIBA). This led to the establishment of the modern architectural profession founded on an approved system of training and accreditation which incorporated features of the earlier system of articled juniors.

Until then builders or other skilled artisans such as Rigg and Levens could describe themselves as 'architects' and produce drawings for their clients. These might be based on published designs which were widespread by the time building started on the Green and certainly by 1886 when the terraces were built at its southern end. In determining the detailed features designers would also be able to consult 'builders' pattern books' used widely by recognised architects.

Of the six qualified architects who designed or advised on houses built on the Green the best known is Stephen Shaw who inherited the architectural practice founded by his father Robert Shaw a designer/builder of the eighteenth century. According to Satchell, Stephen 'built most of the best buildings erected in Kendal between 1870 and the end of the century'[6] working from his offices at 45 Highgate. Houses he designed include his

Stephen Shaw and his wife Jane outside their house at 157 Stricklandgate with their son Malcolm – who was also involved in the design of houses on Kendal Green – and daughter Margaret. She is believed to have taken many of the photographs used in Satchell's 'Family Album', some of which are reproduced in this book.

This composite illustration, of a recent photograph of the two pairs of houses and the elevation drawn by Hodgson in the plans submitted, shows how he intended to join them to enlarge the school to include accommodation for boarders. The elevation also shows that Overdale (24 KG) had been renamed 'St. John's Manse'.

own at 157 Stricklandgate and several on the north side of Queen's Road, as well as *Oakdene*, the grandest house on Kendal Green which was designed in March 1884 for Joseph Jordan. A number of public buildings were to Shaw's design, too, including the Grammar School, the present Town Hall – converted from the old White Hall – and Waterloo House in Finkle Street. Stephen Shaw died in 1930 and is buried in Castle Street Cemetery.[7]

Arthur Hodgson designed for his father, Martin Hodgson, the two pairs of houses, *Silver Howe and Overdale (23 & 24 KG)* and *1 and 2 Holly Croft (25 & 26 KG)* for which plans were approved in 1902 and 1905 respectively. He also drew up the plans in 1913 for the joining of the four houses to make an extended Holly Croft School as mentioned earlier.[8] The ground floor of the extra piece joining them was intended as a gymnasium and the floor above as bedrooms, separated by a corridor joining the teaching rooms in *Holly Croft* and accommodation proposed for boarders in the other two houses. A covered walkway was also planned to connect the two buildings at ground level at the back of the properties.

Born in 1880 Arthur was articled from 1895 to 1900 to the Kendal architect John Curwen, 24 Highgate. Some houses in Aynam and

Burneside roads designed by the Curwen practice together with the public buildings, St. John's Mission and Avenue House, are illustrated on the Kendal Civic Society's chart of Kendal's twentieth century Architecture. Hodgson then worked as an architectural assistant at firms in Nottingham and London until 1904 when he became a partner in a Lincoln firm before establishing his own practice in Windermere in 1908. Two years later he became a licentiate of the RIBA. Hodgson's work includes a garden village in Keswick and various private dwellings throughout Westmorland. He died in 1942.

As noted earlier, the architect, Alfred Nelson, who built and lived at *Holmfield*, is assumed to have designed that house. His architectural practice was listed in trade directories regularly between 1897 and 1925 and is known to have designed and built houses at Kentrigg, two of which also feature on the Kendal Civic Society's chart. These are in a style similar in many respects to the designs of other architects illustrated there, very different from that of his own house on Holme Parrock. According to some of Nelson's descendants he designed and constructed the viewpoint and shelter, nicknamed 'The Mushroom', built on Scout Scar to commemorate the Coronation of George V in 1911. Its site yields a breathtaking panorama across the Lyth Valley, south to Morecambe Bay, west to the Coniston massif, north towards the other Lake District peaks and east to the Pennines.

Nelson's business suffered as a result of the First World War which is probably why he already had a tenant in *Holmfield* in 1924, the year in which he sold the house and moved to another he had built, *The Eaves* at Kentrigg. His joinery workshop was nearby at the Burneside end of Kentrigg and he also owned other land in the area.

Malcolm Shaw, shown on the right in the Shaw family photograph, worked in and later took over the practice of his father, Stephen Shaw, at 45 Highgate listed at that address in trade directories until 1938. Malcolm was a friend of David Dodds who lived at *Oakdene* after Jordan and advised David and his son George when they were planning the design of *The Newlands* built in the garden in 1937; however, it seems from a diary of the event that his advice did not match their needs.

Malcolm Shaw was also involved in the design of low cost housing in the 1920s and 1930s at Underley, mentioned below, as well as Helme Close and Castle Grove.

John Dyson who trained in Shaw's practice was commissioned in 1934 by Ronald Pickles and his fiancée Alice Metcalf to design *Pinewoods* further up Albert Road West from *The Newlands*. In 1947 he was involved in a somewhat bizarre failed planning application to build on the plot of land on which 36 Kendal Green now stands. He wrote a letter supporting a Miss Leggett in her wish to erect a disassembled timber-framed building – previously a café, store and kitchen – which it was hoped to transport to Kendal from Littlehampton in Sussex where it was stored.

Dyson also designed his own, very well specified, house at *44 Kendal Green*, for which planning permission was obtained in May 1936. A drawing of the house appears on the Kendal Civic Society chart. Dyson lived there until at least 1964 but is said to have never got round to completing the house fully in those 28 years. Meanwhile the garden was largely uncontrolled and the ducks which were housed there in an 'ark' also wandered into the house.

Dyson did not have his own architectural practice but worked early on in his career in the Shaws' practice. Then, at about the time his own house was built, he left Shaws to become the first corporation architect employed by the Town Council. In that role he continued work on a project on which the Shaw practice had been engaged, building low cost houses for the Council at Castle Grove; these are also illustrated in the Kendal Civic Society chart. However, whereas the Shaws built in stone Dyson finished off the series in brick to reduce costs, a decision that is said to have upset his previous employer.

The house that Dyson designed and lived in at 44 Kendal Green.

The last house on Kendal Green to be designed by a named architect – Michael Bottomley of Haigh Architects – was *Empson Hill*, completed in December 1964. He joined the Kendal practice of Donald Haigh in Lowther Street in 1949 after graduating from the School of Architecture at Liverpool University. Haigh died in 1953 and his widow, Jean Haigh, invited Bottomley to go into partnership with her in order to keep the practice going. He ran the practice with the help of architects employed there until, in 1990, the Haigh's son, Roger, moved back to

Kendal from the USA, where he had been working as an architect, to become Michael Bottomley's partner.

So-called 'modern' designs, of the sort that David Russell sought for his own family house, *Empson Hill*, were not Michael Bottomley's preferred mode. However, in designing *Empson Hill* he made good use of his understanding of the work of others whose houses were acknowledged as 'modern' within the architectural press. The result was a house that his clients, the Russells, consider is a 'classic' of its period. The only other building Michael Bottomley designed in Kendal which he would class as modern in these terms is the Chapel in Parr Street.

The partners in the Haigh practice are better known for their new work, such as the vicarage of St. Mary's Church, Windermere, and the restoration of buildings and the adaptation of the space within them for new uses. Notable examples in Kendal include the Shakespeare Centre created for use by the community out of the old Theatre of that name, the restoration of Aynam Lodge for use as a conference and training centre and the redevelopment of Kendal railway station into Station House which incorporated some of the original buildings and created space for offices, retail outlets and a doctor's surgery.

CHAPTER VI

THE PEOPLE AND THEIR SOCIAL LIFE

CENSUS COMPARISONS

W E TURN OUR attention now to people who lived on the Green and the lives they lived. Their number had already risen to 46 at the time of the 1871 Census, occupying eleven houses. Ten people lived in *Denmark House* as part of Robert Butterwith's household. The Census of ten years later showed there were still eleven houses occupied with three under construction. Only 39 people lived on the Green then, just four of them in *Denmark House* where the head of household was one John Dodds.

In the 1891 Census data, 35 houses were listed all but one of which were occupied. Of the 34 heads of household 23 were married men and one a bachelor, two spinsters, four widowers and four widows. In total there were 59 children, 26 sons and 33 daughters. In 22 of the households domestic help was available; there were 27 employed in total including 25 listed as 'servants', one as a 'maid' and one as a 'nurse'. In addition there were five boarders or lodgers and one apprentice.

The gender distribution of children at home at various ages in 1891 is perhaps interesting. Between ages 1–15 and 16–21 they were in balance but of those older than 21 who remained at home only one was a man, whereas eight were women.

By the time of the 1901 Census no further houses had been completed but only 33 of the 35 were occupied on the due date.

Of the heads of household 24 were married men and one a bachelor, three widowers and three widows and two spinsters. 71 children lived at home, 32 sons and 39 daughters but their gender distribution differed very little between the ages of 1–21 and over 21. On the other hand, a much higher proportion of children of both sexes aged over 21 lived at home: 31% (22 out of 71) in 1901 compared with 15% (9 out of 59) in 1891. The number of living-in servants had fallen to only 17 (from 27 ten years earlier, including three at the Whitwells, 1 *Fairfield*). However, the number of boarders or lodgers was five, the same as ten years earlier.

BUSINESS PEOPLE

A wide variety of occupations are listed in the four Censuses including many who were employed in business: manufacturers, merchants and retailers as well as their managers, sales representatives and assistants. Others were in land agency, dentistry, journalism and farming.

We start with John Birkett, who owned the first houses to be built on the Green in 1864 at *1–3 Albert Road East* (63–65 KG). It is very likely that this is the John Birkett listed in Census records as a 'carpet weaver of humble origin', born in 1805 and married to Agnes Taylor at an address on House of Correction Hill. This link is supported by the 1904 Rates Book for Kendal Green which shows that the middle house of the terrace was owned by Ann Stubbs (the name of the daughter of the John Birkett referred to in the Census) and the other two houses by George Birkett Stubbs (Ann's son).

The latter was well-known locally as a bespoke tailor, working from his shop at 101 Stricklandgate, called 'The Tower' on the corner of Stricklandgate and Sandes Avenue. George was born and lived for many years at 3 Shaw's Brow, now 55 Windermere Road. Family folklore suggests he was a cripple and used to trundle down to his shop on a trolley but it does not record how he managed to get back home up the steep hill! George was one of the original founders and directors of the Kendal Victoria Bowling Club and a few days prior to his death in 1928 was elected a life member. His gravestone in Parkside Road Cemetery bears the verse:

> 'Afflictions sore long time bore
> Physicians were in vain
> God thought it best that I should go
> And freed me from my pain'.[1]

George Rigg the builder/architect of Birkett's houses lived nearby in another to his own design, 4 *Albert Road East*, until at least 1889; he was listed as 'head of the household' in the 1871, 1881 and 1891 Census returns. He seems to have been a very active resident of the Green, witness for example his protest in 1882 against a Borough requirement under the Public Health Act of 1875, that he should form a 'kerb, footpath and channel' with a 'footwalk of gravel and limestone'. The total cost of its construction along Albert Road East was to be £79-3s-4d of which Rigg's share was £5-9s-2d. His complaint, made in great detail, referred to certain precedents: that 'Kendal Fell Act gives Trustees power to make roads and parapets where required'; that the Trust had maintained a 'parapet' at no charge for fifteen years on both the east and west side; and the Town Surveyor had done similarly along Queen's Road and 'Castle Street by Barley Meadow'.

Rigg was probably also one of those who petitioned the Trustees in 1870 'to rail in the Green, lay out walks and plant trees'. Even so, when it was decided three months later to do something about the trees, the Trustees 'granted a sum of five pounds toward the expense of planting trees' and decided that 'a cheque for that amount be signed in favour of Mr George Rigg'.

Perhaps the best known local businessmen to have rented and owned houses on Kendal Green was Isaac Braithwaite (1844–1929). He and his wife, Mary Snowden, rented *Holly Croft* (25–26 KG) from Martin Hodgson from 1910 to 1914 so that their niece, Kathleen Wilson, could start a girls' school there. The Braithwaites went on to buy the house in 1914 and it remained their property, or that of Isaac Braithwaite's executors, until at least 1931.

From 1914 to 1919 Belgian refugees lived in *Holly Croft* and in the next two houses, *Silver Howe* and *Overdale* (23–24 KG), which were probably rented from Hodgson by the Braithwaites for this purpose. In 1919 *Holly Croft* was renamed St. Monica's and converted to a home for unmarried mothers and was used for that purpose until the early 1930s.

Isaac Braithwaite was the second son of Charles Lloyd Braithwaite who, with his younger brother, George Foster Braithwaite, carried on the family business of drysalters in Highgate and founded a firm of woollen manufacturers. Isaac left school early to join the family business but later spent two years as a student at Edinburgh University where he was awarded a gold medal for his scientific studies. In 1872 he was one of the joint secretaries of the Committee set up to finance through subscription the building of Kendal Green School and in 1911, when working in Birmingham for the greater part of each year, he was a Trustee of the school at the time of the appeal to rebuild it after the fire of the previous year.

For the rest of Isaac Braithwaite's business life, even as a senior partner in the drysaltery and Chairman of Directors of the woollen business, he maintained a keen interest in the latest developments in science, especially chemistry. In 1885 he established Isaac Braithwaite and Son, Engineers, to manufacture and sell equipment for a water heating process he had invented. Although this venture did not prosper the firm continued in business, specialising eventually in the manufacture of laundry machinery. This development influenced the output of the drysaltery which, increasingly, included products for use in commercial laundries.

Of the previous generation of Braithwaites all except his father and an uncle had left the Society of Friends following the schism within its membership referred to earlier. Isaac too became a Quaker and his commitment was strengthened by the support he received from his wife Mary Snowden (née Thomas) of Baltimore.

Isaac met Mary during a visit she made to Kendal in 1878. Even then he was enamoured of her but, on account of business uncertainties, he delayed for many years proposing to her. So it was not until 1890 that they married by which time he was 46. Mary stimulated him to take a much greater part in the affairs of the Society of Friends and of the town, where for some years he was a member of the Council. In 1907, when Isaac was already 63 and his wife 57, they became Wardens of Woodbrooke, established in 1903 as 'The Settlement for Religious and Social Study' in

Isaac and Mary Snowden Braithwaite

Bournville, Birmingham. For each of the seven years in this role they spent two-thirds of the time there and one-third at home in Kendal when Isaac devoted a great deal of time to the family businesses. Even so, they contributed considerably to Woodbrooke's spiritual life, encouraged a large growth in the number of students and sponsored and supervised many additions and improvements to its buildings and other facilities.

In 1911 they moved to Ghyll Close, Greenside, the house built by Isaac's father; there, during the war many Conscientious Objectors came to seek their advice and Isaac published and circulated a pamphlet on the peace question, reflecting his feeling of how wrong the war was and his deep sympathy with those who suffered its consequences.

Shortly after the armistice Mary Snowden started to suffer loss of memory and eventually 'lost her mind' such that, eventually, Isaac had to have nursing care for her. Despite this he remained in good health almost up to his death in 1929.[2]

When Mary died in 1931 her obituary referred to how, on her arrival in Kendal 'she almost took our breath away by her keenness, her vivacity, her stories and the solid, deep, great goodness'.[3]

Much later, the Braithwaite name was again associated with the Green when, in 1951, *Overdale* (24 KG) was bought by Isaac Braithwaite & Son, Drysalters, to provide accommodation for Norman Turvey (1897–1975), company secretary and, later, a director of the firm. He spent twelve happy years there which gave him opportunities to enjoy the Lake District as an enthusiastic walker and cyclist and to take an active part in the activities of the Society of Friends.

Turvey had been a member of the Friends' Ambulance Unit from 1915–1919, the year in which he married Jeanne Marguerite Kaiser in Oberhofen, Alsace, and then returned to England to study accountancy in Birkenhead before joining the shipbuilders, Alfred Holt & Co. In 1927 he moved to the post of bursar at Ackworth School where his mother had been a pupil. After nineteen years there he was appointed secretary and a governor of Royal Wanstead School prior to taking up his post with Braithwaites. On Turvey's retirement in 1962 he and Jeanne settled in Great Chesterford, Essex, where he died in 1975.[4]

John Thomas Illingworth was an early resident of the Green, a tobacco and snuff manufacturer who owned and lived at 2 *Fernlea*. At some stage in his career he worked for the firm of Brocklebank and Gawith before starting his own company, J.T. Illingworth & Sons, one of three that survived into the twentieth century, along with two owned by members of the Gawith family. When Illingworth died, the firm was taken over by his son,

James, who lived at *3 Beechwood* during the early 1890s. His wife, Mary Agnes, was a daughter of Robert Butterwith of *Denmark House*. Illingworths closed down in 1983 after the company's Aynam Mills burned down.

Samuel Henry Gawith who lived at *Holmfield* was a member of the family involved in the other two firms that survived. Both stemmed from the company, Brocklebank and Gawith, into which his grandfather, the first Samuel Gawith (Kendal Fell Trustee, 1861–65), was taken into partnership by Brocklebank on the death of his partner Harrison, Gawith's father-in-law. When Brocklebank died in about 1850 Gawith continued to run the firm as Samuel Gawith and Company until, on his death, it was taken over by his sons, Samuel II and John. They fell out over a law suit and split the company: Samuel took the snuff mill at Meal Bank and John the factory in Lowther Street. At some point, when John became bankrupt, Samuel bought the goodwill of his firm, but not the premises and equipment, and moved to Canal Head.

The Gawith Hoggarth sign on the wall of the company's premises in Lowther Street.

In 1887, the youngest of the seven Gawith brothers, William Gawith – known as Henry – founded the firm of Gawith Hoggarth Co. at 27, Lowther Street in partnership with Henry Hoggarth. They took over the redundant equipment and used the mill at Helsington to grind their snuff. Some years after his death the firm passed to his son Samuel Henry who joined the family firm as a youth and was still its chairman at the time of his death in 1966, aged 74.[5]

Samuel Henry was the son-in-law of Alfred Nelson from whom, in 1924, he bought *Holmfield* where he lived for thirty years during which time many much-acclaimed Christmas parties were hosted there.

At least three residents of the Green were associated with the wine merchants and brewers, Whitwell Marks and Company, including the owner of *1 Fairfield*, Edward Whitwell, 1817–1893. He was the younger brother of John Whitwell, 1811–1880, the Kendal Fell Trustee mentioned earlier who ran a carpet factory at Dockwray Mill. They were two of eight children of Isaac and Hannah Maria Whitwell all of whom were born in the former town house of the Wilsons of Dallam Tower at 118 Highgate, later used as the brewery office.[6]

The original licence to sell wines at this Highgate address was granted to a member of the Whitwell family in 1758. The business grew under the direction of members of the Whitwell family until early in the following century when a partnership was formed with William Mark. He managed the brewing side of the business while Whitwell looked after the wine trade. In 1850 the partnership was dissolved and the business split into two concerns with Whitwell continuing to deal in wine and Mark running the brewery. New brewery buildings were built eight years later, sited in the gardens behind the Highgate house. Then in 1883 the business was incorporated as a private limited liability company in the name of Whitwell, Mark and Co. Ltd. One of the joint managing directors was Wallis Evershed who in the 1891 Census was listed as a 'brewery and analytical chemist' residing with his family at 2 *Beechwood Terrace*. By 1894 he had moved to the house owned by the company at 122 Highgate where he died in 1911.

The management of the company was taken over in 1910 by Arthur

Photograph of Brewery staff taken in 1910, the year in which Arthur Miles took over the company; he is seated fourth from the left in the front row. A very large print of the photograph is displayed in the Brewery Arts Centre.

An engraving of Jordan's Granary taken from one of the company's bill heads dated 16 February 1891.

Miles who, prior to that, had been the company's accountant. Born in Dorset he was crippled from childhood as a result of a serious knee injury but went on to train as an accountant. He worked in this role for a brewery in Lichfield before taking up the post in Kendal. Miles is credited with reviving the fortunes of Whitwell Mark after its business had suffered in the face of increased competition and a decline in beer drinking nationally. In 1915 he was taken into partnership and in 1929 became the sole proprietor of the business and chairman of its executive committee.

In the rate books for 1910 and a directory published two years later Miles was listed as resident at 2 *Fairbank*, still owned by David Pennington. By 1918 he and his family – like the Eversheds before them – were living at 122 Highgate where they stayed until 1924, when they moved to Milnthorpe. Arthur Miles died in 1944 aged 67 and two years later the company was acquired from his Executors by Vaux and Scottish and Newcastle Breweries. In about 1946 Mrs Miles and her children moved back to Kendal where they lived at 26 Kendal Green.

The brewery continued in operation until the 18th September 1968, when the final brew of 'Auld Kendal' was made and the firm closed, the last in Westmorland. In 1970 the buildings were acquired by the Lake District Art Gallery Trust for conversion to the Brewery Arts Centre; the Georgian House on Highgate became a Youth Hostel.

Joseph Jordan who had *Oakdene* built for his family in 1884 was owner of J. Jordan and Sons, Corn and Flour Dealers. Stephen Shaw, the architect for the house, designed in 1887 two commercial buildings for Jordan's firm: a massive granary which dominated Allhallows Lane from its prime position between Low Fell Side and Beast Banks, and a shop on three storeys with hoist for loading merchandise. The granary was demolished in 1971 to make way for blocks of housing which now step up the steep slope whereas the shop still stands, its façade largely unchanged, at 1 Allhallows Lane just off Stricklandgate. The shop was used for the sale of pork and hams as well as grain products.

Alexander Armstrong who lived at 15 Kendal Green (9 *Beechwood Terrace*) for at least the period from 1934 to 1975 is believed to have been a supervisor at the granary. Recently, in the garden of that house a sign board was found with the name 'J. Jordan and Sons' in bright gold lettering against a deep green background. Metal rings attached to the board suggest that it hung on the side of a cart or other vehicle.

The carpet industry was also represented on the Green. From 1891 until at least 1924, Vincent Salvator Smith, a carpet designer, born in Kidderminster, lived at 10 *Beechwood*.

David Dodds and his son George sitting on the steps at Oakdene.

A generation later David Dodds also moved up from Kidderminster in the early 1920s to reintroduce carpet making into Kendal just a century after it had started up. It was then that he bought *Oakdene* where he lived with his wife Mary Ramsey (née Waldie) and son George Waldie.

Dodds began his management career in the carpet industry in Kirkcaldy then moved to become a factory manager for a Kidderminster firm in 1902. In 1919 he resigned his post there in order to bring back into commission the carpet mill in Highgate that had been under the direction of J.H. Braithwaite and Richard Nelson until it was closed down in 1914. The equipment from the earlier mill was transferred at that time to Meal Bank which gave Dodds the opportunity to introduce modern machinery when he purchased the buildings. Although there were many men in Kendal who had worked in the carpet industry, including some who had moved up from Kidderminster in the 1880s, when the factory reopened in 1922 the weaving was done by women and girls.[7]

In 1928 Highgate Mill was bought by the Lancaster firm of Wm. Goodacre and Sons at which point D. & G. Dodds was incorporated with Goodacre, and David and his son George Dodds became directors of the new firm. Five years later the company bought Castle Mills, just across the

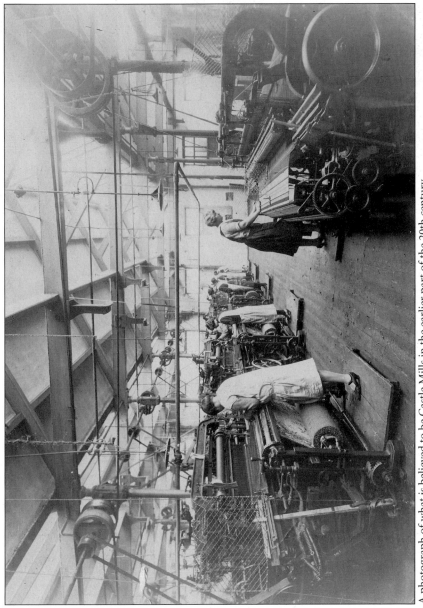

A photograph of what is believed to be Castle Mills in the earlier part of the 20th century.

river from Highgate, in order to manufacture narrowloom Axminster carpeting. The introduction of new machinery was overseen by David and George.[8]

Also in textiles were the Harrisons who lived on the Green, Rupert Harrison at *Overdale* (24 KG) from 1923 to 1951 and his brother, Hal, at *Highfield* (50 KG, then called *Highfield House*) from at least 1924 to 1938. They took over from their father, Henry, the running of H. Harrison and Sons which dealt in hosiery and woollen goods from a warehouse in New Road. At an earlier stage in its history the firm included a mill at Crook which specialised in making pitmen's stockings. Before he died Henry persuaded Hal to give up a banking career to partner Rupert in the firm. Rupert specialised in marketing and selling while Hal looked after the office side.

Rupert's wife, Annie, was a daughter of William Alexander who ran J. Alexander and Sons, a firm of wine and spirit merchants, brewers and aerated water manufacturers founded by William's father, Jonas Alexander. The brewery and factory were on Beezon Road, bordering the river between Stramongate and Sandes Avenue, and the wine and spirit merchants was on Finkle Street.

Alfred Crossley, who brought his family to live at 5 *Wood Lea* in 1919, ran the brush manufacturers, Rainforth Hodgson, which had developed from a business started by Grant and Hodgson in 1838. He began his

Engraving of Rainforth Hodgson advertisement of 1953 showing the Blackhall Brush Factory.

career as an apprentice to his uncle, Henry Tedcastle, who is believed to
have owned the company with one of the Braithwaite family. Rainforth
Hodgson was then in premises at Black Hall on Stricklandgate, a historic
building where Henry Wilson had lived, the first Alderman to be
appointed under the town's Charter granted by Queen Elizabeth in 1575.
The Wilson family owned Black Hall until 1733 when it passed by marriage to a family named Standish who lived
there until 1869 when it was sold to
Rainforth Hodgson for £650.[9]

The site is still signified by a black, bris-
tled hog mounted on the wall above what
is now the Halifax Estate Agency. This is a
copy of the original hog which is in the
Museum of Lakeland Life and Industry at
Abbot Hall.

At some stage Alfred Crossley bought
Illingworth's tobacco factory in Sandes
Avenue, the address on the advertisement
shown opposite, so as to have bigger premises in which to carry out manufacturing. Black Hall was kept as a retail outlet and storage until the
1950s.

In his role as owner/director Alfred was assisted by his son, George
who, in 1945, moved with his family to live at *10 Kendal Green* (earlier *4
Beechwood*) only five doors away from his father. When Alfred died ownership of the company passed to Mrs Crossley at which point George and
his daugher, Hilda, who was already involved with the firm, took over its
management. When George himself died from the effects of a bee sting in
1960, aged 53, Hilda kept the business going until the last of the early
apprentices reached retirement age when the company closed.

Alfred's immediate neighbours at *6 Wood Lea* were James and
Josephine Ruthven, long-standing residents of the Green. After James was
killed in a motorcycle accident Mrs Ruthven continued to live in the
house. Then, in later years, the Crossleys had a bell installed that linked
their bedroom to hers so that she could summon help if needed.

Many other residents of the Green ran firms which provided various
services or retail businesses. Robert and Charles Butterwith, for example,
ran a grocery for many years when living, successively, at *Denmark House*.
A bizarre accident happened in Charles' household in 1896 when his
eleven year old great-nephew, who lived with the family, shot a 'maid servant called Isabella Nelson' in the head. 'Fortunately three doctors were

summoned immediately and poor Isabella's head was trepanned in the house. No anaesthetic was used and the patient was held down by Mrs Butterwith and the Misses Butterwith but Isabella apparently recovered from her ordeal'.[10]

Albert Pickles, who lived at *Denmark House* from 1919 to 1960 was proprietor of Kendal Steam Laundry in Wildman Street. In 1929 the firm was taken over by Lakeland Laundries Limited who set up a factory on Shap Road now occupied by Sunlight Service Group. Albert's son Ronald Pickles, who lived at *Pinewoods* from 1937, suffered severe spinal problems from the age of 19 which prevented him from continuing his chosen career in banking. Instead he started working as office manager in his father's business. When, due to ill health, Ronald took early retirement from Lakeland Laundry in 1953, his wife, Alice, joined her mother in running the haberdashery, Metcalfs, at 108 Stricklandgate.

After surviving a house fire in 1996 that cost the insurance company £50,000 in repairs, Ronald and Alice died within a few months of each other during the next year: he was 91 and she 90, and had lived at *Pinewoods* for 61 years. Their daughter, Janet, inherited the house but, having settled elsewhere in England, sold it in December 1997 to Norman and Ann Ellis who had for a number of years helped the Pickles in the garden and in other ways around the house as they became more frail.[11]

In Finkle Street in the twentieth century there were three shops run by people related by birth and/or marriage all of whom lived on the Green: the Blacows, the Brennands and the Dodds. James Charles Blacow, who owned *Laurel Mount* (19 KG) during the period 1925 to 1953, ran Blacow Bros., the family firm of men's outfitters in Finkle Street. The business was taken over by his son, James Lewis ('Jim'), on returning home from war service. In 1947 Jim married Rene Stables and in 1963 they bought *Oakdene*, two doors from *Laurel Mount*, and lived there until 1974. Jim Blacow died in 1993 aged 71 while playing golf at Kendal Golf Club.

James Charles Blacow was married to Bertha Brennand whose family ran a pork butchers in Finkle Street. The premises are still owned by the family, but run independently by tenants as 'The Food Hall'; on its plate glass window is an advertisement in large gold letters for Brennands. Further down Finkle Street was an ironmongers run by George Dodds, who inherited *Oakdene* from his father David, and his wife Dorothy, daughter of James Charles Blacow; they maintained the name, Bailie and Hargreaves, to take advantage of its reputation around Kendal. The Brennands also had a shop in Stricklandgate probably where 'Lakeland' is now.

An early photograph of Blacow's shop in Finkle Street.

Bertha Blacow's brother, George Brennand, lived at 55 Kendal Green which has an unusual bay window for the display of goods for sale. In a 1953 directory it was listed as *The Beeches*, a boarding house, with those living there shown as Mrs Brennand and Gilbert Brennand.

F. W. Boon, the Chemists, was run by Frank Boon who owned and lived at *2 Fairbank* (18 KG) in the period 1924 – 1931 and had tenants there until 1936. His son Jack worked in the shop until ill health forced him to retire when, in turn, his son John took over. The premises were on the corner of Market Place and Stricklandgate, now Greenwoods the tailors.

The shop was never modernised and retained its original mahogany drawers with their Latin labels. On a small gas ring in the cellar cough mixtures and syrups were made in black enamelled cauldron-like vessels. Boon's was also a veterinary chemist, in which Jack Boon specialised. This side of the business involved the sale of various treatments, including horse liniment, mostly made on the premises in huge steel drums. Another specialism was hound and puppy trail which 'Mr Jack' would decant into second-hand wine bottles, before corking and then sealing them with red wax.

Very well known to the people of Kendal was a large model rat, 2 to 3 feet long, which would make its appearance in the side window of Boons

COAL.   **JAMES WHARTON & SON,**   **COAL.**

COLLIERY AGENTS, COAL & COKE MERCHANTS,

18, MARKET PLACE, KENDAL.

District Agents to Messrs, Pease & Partners, Ltd., Darlington, and West Houghton Coal and Cannel Co., Ltd., West Leigh and Byron Holt Collieries.

St. HELENS. Best Coal.

TINDALE. do.

The above St. Helens and Tindale are the finest seams of Coal in the Durham Coal Fields, owned by Pease and Partners, are good sample, well screened, big and bright, hot and durable, and by far the most economical Coal to the consumer.

SILKSTONE HARDS. The celebrated real Silkstone from the Silkstone Collieries are a splendid sample, big, no small, largely used, give every satisfaction.

WALLSEND. From the Castle Wallsend Collieries, large sample, bright, free burning.

WALLSEND. From Wigan District, good, clean burning Coal.

CRIPPIN'S ROUND ARLEY. One of the finest samples from the Wigan District, recommended as good all round household Coal.

LONG ARLEY. This is a good Coal but rather soft, cakes together, makes a good, bright fire.

BICKERSHAW. This is an excellent second class Coal, free burning, very hot, splendid cooking Coal, clean, burns all away.

PEMBERTON. Good cottage kitchen Coal, nice sample, not so large, burns to brown ash.

CROMBOKE. Larger sample than Pemberton, free burning, hot Coal, grey ashes, good, useful Coal.

PEASE'S COKES for all purposes.

  ,, **STEAM FUEL** of all descriptions.

  ,, **NUTS & PEAS** for smith's use.

    All well screened and ricked.

The above can be obtained at the depots, Railway Station, Kendal.

Carted in Town or Country or supplied in truck loads to any Station. Orders addressed to 18, Market Place, or to the office at the depot, will have every attention.

TRIAL SOLICITED.

PRICES ON APPLICATION.

18, MARKET PLACE, KENDAL.

Wharton's advertisement in the 1895 brochure for the Grand Oriental Bazaar in support of Kendal Green School. These were the days when 'Coal was King' and came in many guises.

at certain times of the year as an advertisement for 'Warfarin'. The shop remained open until the 1980s.[12]

James Wharton, a coal merchant, owned 6 *Beechwood* (12 KG) and lived there during the period 1894 to 1897, but continued to own the house until at least 1932. By 1901 Mrs Matilda Tipper had become his tenant. Wharton's business interest extended beyond coal as shown by his purchase in 1920 of the Maltkiln on Caroline Street for use as a furniture warehouse.

Finally, among the businessmen who lived on the Green, was the auctioneer and accountant Theodore DeRome. He and his family lived at 4 *Beechwood* (10 KG) for at least the period from 1891 to 1904 and in 1889 he acted on behalf of the 'Kendal Green Protection Association' in dealing with the Kendal Fell Trust.

After an early education at Stramongate School Theodore trained with a London firm of auctioneers and accountants and then started a business in Lancaster. He gave this up in 1878 to join his father, Matthew, in his firm of auctioneers founded in 1854. On passing his examinations to become a chartered accountant, the firm's name was changed to 'M. DeRome and Son'.

On the death of his father in 1903 he became sole proprietor of the firm which continued to thrive and went on to manage many major auctions in the area working both for private clients and government

DeRome's offices at
21 Stramongate.

agencies. Apart from his business life Theodore DeRome had few other
interests although he attended the Friend's Meeting House and was a very
keen angler. He died in 1911 at his house, Aikrigg End, Kendal.[13]

CHURCHMEN AND PUBLIC SERVANTS

Other notable people have lived on the Green who were not in business or
manufacturing. Among them were ministers and clergymen of local
churches and numerous public servants well known in the local community to which they contributed.

Records show that churchmen lived in at least six houses from early in
the twentieth century. The Census of 1901 lists Herbert Kelsey, a Church
of England clergyman, as lodging with Sarah Robson at 4 *Wood Lea* (4

The Rev. Gray in charge of a stall at the Garden Sale held at Rosemont, Burneside Road on 18 July 1907 in aid of St. John's Presbyterian Church.

KG) and from 1904–1906 the Rev. Marshall Gray, minister of St. John's United Presbyterian Church in Sandes Avenue, lived at 2 *Fairfield* (29 KG). St. John's was built in 1897 to a design by Stephen Shaw and it was his daughter, Margaret, who presented Mr Gray, and his wife, with books when he left the church.

After Gray's departure visiting ministers preached at St. John's until 1912 when Rev. Scott Hendry became minister. Again Margaret Shaw was involved in the preparations for his induction and the reception that followed it. In 1913 Hendry was living at *Overdale* (24 KG) which, as noted earlier, had been renamed *St John's Manse*. It is not known what became of him when the Belgian refugees were housed there from 1914–1919 but he is listed as living back in *Overdale* again in 1921.

From 1910 a stream of ministers of Stricklandgate Methodist Church were resident at *Holly Bank (20 KG)* starting with Rev. John Hardcastle who was followed by William George (1914), John Ward (1921), Frederick Mann (1925), Albert Yorke (1930) and Robert Armstrong (1934–38). Armstrong is believed to have started the Wesleyan Chapel at Longpool.

A Methodist minister, Rev. Williams, lived at *10 Beechwood* (16 KG) in the period 1934–38 and a retired minister, Rev. T. E. Bellis, owned *3 Beechwood* for at least part of that time.

Many of the public servants who lived on the Green over the years were involved in education including Charles Tipper. At the age of 29, when he lived with his widowed mother, Matilda, at *6 Beechwood*, Charles was listed in the 1901 Census as 'Organising Secretary, Technical Education'. In 1906 he lived in Greenside, then rented *Highfield* (50 KG) from at least 1910 to 1914 and in 1921 was living at Bridge House, Castle Street. By 1919 he had been appointed Director, Westmorland Education Committee, a position he still held in 1934. Tipper was also closely involved with the Allen Technical Institute, previously the Technical School, designed by Stephen Shaw, and opened in 1914.

Another key figure in local education was William Gardiner, Headmaster of Kendal Green School, who lived at *4 Wood Lea* for at least sixteen years until 1897. Born in North Devon in 1860 he won a scholarship to Westminster Training College in 1879 after which he taught at a National Children's Home and Orphanage School near Bolton. Gardiner was appointed Head Master at Kendal in 1884 where he remained until 1925. In that period he steered the school through its expansion phase in the 1890s and was a key figure in ensuring that it recovered from the fire of 1910.

Kendal Green School soccer team 1921–22. William Gardiner is standing back left.

Gardiner died aged 80 in 1940 when living at 21 Highfield Villas on Windermere Road his home since at least 1906.[14] When the school buildings were converted for residential use almost fifty years later they were named Gardiner Bank in his honour. Though William Gardiner was prominent in the Stricklandgate Methodist Church his two daughters were teachers at the Quaker School in Stramongate.

Amelia Anderson was infants mistress at Kendal Green School including the period 1910 to 1914, when Gardiner was headmaster. In the 1901 Census, at *7 Beechwood*, she was already shown as 'schoolmistress', living with her parents who were tenants in the house, and two sisters, Rachel and Evelyn, also teachers. The latter was still a tenant there in 1938 aged about 64.

In the 1881 Census two sisters, Isabella and Elizabeth Nicholson, listed as schoolmistresses, are shown as living with their brother at *3 Albert Road East* (63 KG). As mentioned earlier they bought 1 Airethwaite in which they ran a very successful school.

Kathleen Mary Wilson, a Quaker, was headmistress of Holly Croft

School for girls from 1910 to 1914. She was born in 1882, the third child and only daughter of Thomas Crewdson Wilson and his wife Anna Mary, née Braithwaite. As a young girl she was known as Lena when the family lived at 5 Bankfield, a terrace on the south side of Greenside. In 1889, two years after her mother died, the family – father, Kathleen and her three brothers – moved to live with her aunt and uncle, Isaac and Mary Snowden Braithwaite who extended their house, Castle Lodge, to accommodate them. Isaac acted as a second father to the children and the three nephews worked with him in business. Later Kathleen lived with the Braithwaites at *Ghyll Close*, Greenside, where they had moved in 1911 following the death of Isaac's father who built the house; from 1931 she had a flat in a part of the house.

Kathleen was educated at the Girls' School in Stramongate from 1889 to 1896 when she moved on to the High School. From there she became a student of Westfield College, London University, graduating with a BA Degree and a Certificate in Teaching in 1905. Two years later she returned to Stramongate as a teacher in the Girls' School at a salary of £90 per annum. When the girl's school was closed in 1910 she started a new school in *Holly Croft* (25 & 26KG) where she intended to continue the Stramon-

Isaac and Mary Braithwaite with the Wilson family in the garden of Castle Lodge in the early 1900s. Kathleen is kneeling in front.

gate tradition of girls' education. At that time the house was rented by her uncle and aunt, Isaac and Mary Snowden Braithwaite.

Kathleen was assisted by two teachers Winifred Hird and Constance Bright who taught, respectively, modern languages and art. Like Kathleen, both had taught previously at Stramongate School.

According to the School brochure it offered 'a thorough grounding in all branches of English, *very special attention* being paid in the Lower Forms to Reading, Writing, Spelling and Composition'. Various branches of mathematics, French and Latin, with German and Greek were also taught as options, as were science including physiology, hygiene and nature study, a wide range of handicrafts and physical exercises which extended to 'Swedish Drill' and cricket. Music lessons were optional, taken by a visiting master or mistress.

Pupils were prepared for examinations under the Junior and Senior Oxford Local Board and the Royal Drawing Society and, at more advanced levels, for Matriculation or for Cambridge Higher Local Examinations.

Various other provisions were made including the allocation of plots in the 'good garden' of the house where those who wished could practise gardening; educational excursions by carriage to local places of interest; and 'good cloakroom accommodation, with heating arrangements for wet weather'. A luncheon room was available for pupils coming from a distance, for whom the Caretaker provided hot water, or made tea, cocoa etc. as desired.

In 1914, the year in which Isaac and Mary Braithwaite purchased *Holly Croft*, a larger illustrated brochure was published advertising Kathleen Wilson's intention to extend the school by joining *Silver Howe and Overdale (23 & 24 KG)*, to allow for room for boarders. Presumably this was done with the agreement of Martin Hodgson who still owned these other houses and whose architect son drew plans for them to be joined to *Holly Croft* to house the expanded school.

The brochure includes photographs of pupils at their studies, presumably during the previous four years. Eleven sit at desks in an upper bedroom of what is now 26 Kendal Green, eight are at work in 'the studio' on a lower floor and, in a 'kindergarten' on the ground floor, nine younger children are engaged in various activities. Unlike the 1910 brochure, which makes no mention of Kathleen Wilson's Quaker background, it is emphasised in the new one that the School 'is under the care of members of the Society of Friends, and seeks to carry on the traditions of the Kendal Girls' School established in 1698'.

Sadly, shortly after putting out the new prospectus, the wife of

Kathleen's eldest brother, Charles, died, and she decided that she would give up the school to look after him and his young son. For the rest of her life she devoted herself to the Society of Friends – including the Old Girls' Association of Stramongate School – the British Women's Temperance Association and her home at *Ghyll Close* where she died in 1970.[15]

Another teacher, Edmund Brockbank lived at *Lynton* (46 KG) from some time after plans for it were agreed in 1925 until at least 1953. On a plaque in Queen Katherine's School Brockbank is commemorated as being headteacher of Longlands School from 1916 to 1953. This refers to a succession of council schools that preceded the boys' school of that name opened on the Longlands site – where Queen Katherine's stands – in 1960. These earlier schools include the 'British School' for senior pupils in Castle Street transferred in 1936 to the buildings of the former Friends' School in Stramongate. Whilst serving as a headmaster Brockbank was also chief organiser of the Allen Technical Institute in which practical classes were held during the school day.

John Johnson, a woodwork and metalwork master at Longlands school, was a near neighbour, at 49a Kendal Green. In 1955 Johnson and his wife, Edna, bought the plot from the Borough of Kendal and, despite the steeply sloping site, built the house themselves over the next two years or so. John lived there until his death in 1966; two years later Edna died and the house was sold.

Two other teachers, Alan and Dawn Sutcliffe, lived next door in No. 49b which they bought in 1965. Alan taught at Charlotte Mason College, Dawn at St. Thomas' School which was relocated into the new building nearby in 1966.

Alongside Brockbank's house lived yet another teacher, William Thomas Floyd who owned *Hale Cote* (45 KG) between 1931 and 1974. In 1928 he was teaching at Kendal Green School but later became headmaster of St. Thomas' School. In his retirement speech after thirty years in that position Floyd is reported as saying that 'classes are as large as ever, but in the old days discipline was maintained by fear, but nowadays children enjoy school'.[16]

Others in public service included Harry Martindale the County Treasurer who owned *3 Fairfield* and lived there from at least 1871 until 1894. Much later, Miss Emily Reed, lived at 5 Albert Road East from 1928–1971 during which time she became an Alderman and Mayor of Kendal.

Mary Regan (1912–1986) was another woman who was active in politics during a similar period, 'well known in Kendal for her unstinting work for the people of the town'. In 1967/8 she moved into the ground-floor flat at 30a Kendal Green when prevented by arthritis from climbing stairs. She lived there until 1985 – by which time she had been confined to a wheelchair for several years – and died the following year not long after moving to Stone Cross Nursing Home.

Mary Regan worked as a clerk at Provincial Insurance and her husband, Tony, was a turner at Gilbert, Gilkes and Gordon. Her work as an

independent member of Kendal Borough Council and Westmorland County Council, and the many, less visible, roles she played in her attempt to provide a better life for those who were needy or otherwise vulnerable, is commemorated on a plaque commissioned by Gladys Airey, sited at the Aynam Road end of the footbridge over the river from Abbot Hall.

Patrick O'Neil, nicknamed 'Pat', who lived at *Highfield* for some years after 1938 was Chief Constable of Kendal's police force from 1922 until 1947 when county and borough police forces were amalgamated. According to Bingham, O'Neil was 'an extremely tall man, about 6 feet 4 inches, and as he made his way… up Lowther Street to the Borough Police Station beneath the Town Hall his stylish blue uniform laced with white braid and Field Marshall's epaulettes, Sam Brown belt and much silver on the peak of his cap made him a figure of awe'.[17] People who live on the Green tell of relatives who felt more than awe as O'Neil clipped them around the ear for riding their bikes on the pavement!

TWO WRITERS

A very unusual public servant, Alfred Wainwright, lived at 38 Kendal Green; unusual because he is likely to remain the best known of all its residents to people outside the town, in the UK and abroad, not for his public service but his fame as a writer.

Born in 1907 he spent much of his later life in Kendal following his appointment in 1941 to the Borough Treasurer's Department. Seven years later, in the year he was promoted to Borough Treasurer, Wainwright bought land from Samuel Henry Gawith right at the top of the Green,

Chief Constable Pat O'Neil leads a group of policemen in the Mayor's Sunday Parade in the late 1930s.

Alfred Wainwright, Borough Treasurer, front row centre, with other members of his department. Percy Duff, who succeeded Wainwright as Treasurer, is on his left.

next to Gawith's own house, *Holmfield*. Architect's drawings were approved the following year but the house may not have been completed for the Wainwrights to occupy until 1950. The people who bought the house following Wainwright's death in 1991 extended the house considerably.

The move to Kendal enabled Wainwright to explore the Lake District fells for which he had already developed a passion. Out of this he created 59 books including seven highly acclaimed Pictorial Guides to Lakeland Fells, twenty books on miscellaneous topics – including *Kendal in the 19th Century* – and five books of Lakeland mountain drawings. In 1972 Wainwright devised the Coast to Coast Walk for which his guide was published the following year. He lived at 38 Kendal Green for 41 years until his death in 1991 at which time Mrs Wainwright sold the house.

Another writer, but also a journalist, was John Watson who, in 1885, was living at *1 Fern Lea* with his elder sisters Margaret and Sarah, who owned the house, and their younger sister Edith. *Fern Lea* is also the address shown on John's marriage certificate when he wed Emily Farrer in September 1888. By that time he had become a member of the Society of Friends.

In his boyhood Watson became keenly interested in the natural history of the Lake District fostered by extended holidays in Longsleddale. While still a teenager he became a regular contributor of articles on natural history to the Westmorland Gazette; later his work was published in 'Cornhill' and 'The Field'. So, although he trained as a teacher, his youthful hobby, linked to a facility for writing, enabled Watson to build up a reputation as a journalist.

During his lifetime Watson wrote a number of journal articles and books, the latter including 'The English Lake District Fisheries', 'British Sporting Fishes' and 'Confessions of a Poacher'. On 5th December 1889 he was elected a Fellow of the Linnean Society.

In 1888 Watson founded and became proprietor of Northern Newspaper Syndicates in partnership with a Mr Ernest Taylor. In time the syndicate established connections with newspapers in the UK, the colonies and the USA. Sometime between 1910 and 1914 Watson took over as proprietor and publisher of Kendal Mercury and Times and may have been responsible for changing its name to Westmorland Mercury and Times in 1913. Perhaps this was done to compete with the only other one still published, the Westmorland Gazette and Kendal Advertiser. In any case the

Mercury and Times ceased publication in 1917 leaving the Gazette as the only local newspaper.

Watson was also active in public life, elected in 1889 to the newly created Westmorland County Council, elevated in 1910 to the position of Alderman and then appointed as magistrate in 1914. In his roles as Councillor and Alderman his chief interest lay in the prevention of river pollution and protection of wild birds.

John Watson died in 1928, aged 70, at his home, *Eden Mount*, Horncop Lane just round the corner from Kendal Green.[18]

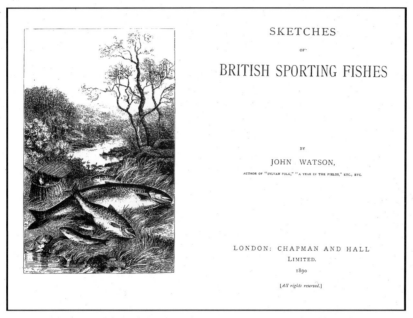

Title page of Watson's book 'Sketches of British Sporting Fishes' published in 1890.

STEAM-BOAT DESIGNER

Charles Fildes was another remarkable person to have lived on Kendal Green. Born into a Manchester family of copper and zinc packing case manufacturers and authorised gas fitters, he became a tin plate manufacturer and pioneer of the use of steam boats on inland lakes. Charles and his family were the first residents of *Overdale* (24 KG) from 1904 – when Fildes was 70 – until 1912. Prior to that they had lived for many years at

Charles Fildes standing on 'Fairy Queen'

Gillbank, Hawkshead where, by 1891, he and his third wife were caring for nine children, the youngest a baby, the oldest aged 22 years.

Fildes' reputation as a pioneer in the use of steam boats on Windermere hinged on his building of 'Fairy Queen', the first private paddle steamer to be used on the lake.[19] The photograph of Fildes on the boat is said to have been taken in about 1859 when he could have been only twenty-one.

Six years later he was reported to be carrying out trials on Esthwaite Water, near his home at Gillbank, of a steamer called 'City of Manchester'. An article in the Westmorland Gazette expressed the horror of one of its correspondents for whom the boat was the 'very hemlock of picturesque depravity'. As duck, coot and waterhen are 'sailing out from among the nodding reads and tufted bullrushes... and as the plumed and stately heron shook her silver plumage in the sun – Oh! murder – yonder comes the black-hulled City of Manchester throwing out volumes of stinking smoke, to deaden the sweet perfume of ten thousand incense-scented wild flowers that grow upon the verdant shores of the much-loved lake'.[20] Perhaps this was the prototype of a steam launch – called, ironically, 'Cygnet' – which Fildes is said to have built after 'Fairy Queen'.

At Sawrey near to Gillbank Charles Fildes owned land where he built a three-foot gauge railway on which a locomotive named 'Lavinia' hauled timber. At that time he continued to work in Manchester at Baxendales taking the train from Windermere. According to his son, Arthur, he rode to the Station on his tricycle.

Charles continued to ride a tricycle after moving to Kendal Green but also had the motor tricycle pictured earlier. Nothing else is known about his life except a record of a visit he made to see Arthur Simpson, the carver and furniture designer, at his house 'Littleholme', Sedbergh Road in August 1910 when Fildes was 76.

Mrs Fildes was a close friend of Margaret Shaw, daughter of Stephen Shaw who designed *Oakdene*. Margaret is believed to have taken many of the photographs – including those of Charles on his tricycles and Mrs Fildes with two of her daughters in the garden of *Overdale* – that prompted the publication of, and illustrate, the book from which this information is taken. In her diaries Margaret Shaw records numerous activities she and Mrs Fildes took part in; altogether she gives an impression of her friend's popularity as a 'hostess' whose 'New Year's Eve party in 1912 went on until 2 a.m.'.[21]

Mrs Fildes died in 1943 aged 88.

Mrs Fildes takes tea with her daughters at Overdale (24 KG), 1905.

MUSICIAN

Another unusual resident of Kendal Green was Eric Nicholson, musician, listed in the 1901 Census as Frederick Will, aged nine, living at 5 *Beechwood* with his father, also Frederick, Secretary of a public company, and his mother, Ada. Presumably he became known as Eric to distinguish him from his father.

Some claim he became an eccentric, a view backed up, for example, by tales of how he always wore a rucksack wherever he went. At least one person who followed his example was Michael Crossley who lived next door (now 10 Kendal Green). As a teenager in the 1950s, Michael struck up a friendship with Eric, much admiring him, especially his musicianship. As a mark of his admiration he too donned a rucksack, a custom maintained to this day when it is much more common. But Michael was drawn to Eric mainly on account of his considerable musical ability and skills, as performer and teacher, from which his young friend was to benefit considerably.

Early on Nicholson showed considerable promise on the piano and violin, confirmed during his training at the Royal Manchester School of Music under the famous Russian violinist Adolph Brodsky, the School's director. He obtained teaching and performance diplomas on both instruments. On his 21st birthday Eric played with the Hallé Orchestra while still a student and in his last term at the School was offered the leadership of the orchestra. Determined to be a soloist he declined the offer in order to continue studying with Brodsky.

As he worked to improve his technique to further his ambition Nicholson suffered problems with his hands. The condition gradually worsened despite the efforts of various specialists to diagnose the problem and propose a cure, although at some later time it seems to have been diagnosed as arthritis. After four fruitless years of practice in Manchester, he gave up on his dream and returned to Kendal to live with his mother who was then a widow.

Eric remained a bachelor and made a living teaching the violin and piano at independent schools around Kendal and by taking a few adult pupils. The brochure he had printed to advertise the lessons listed various referees including Sir Samuel Scott, of *Yews*, Windermere who ran the Provincial Insurance Company started by his father, Sir James. Another referee was Charles Tipper who, as noted above, was Director of the Westmorland Education Committee. The brochure also contained copies of letters of commendation written in February 1916 by Brodsky and Walter Carroll, a Professor in the Royal Manchester College of Music. At the back of the brochure were extracts from various newspapers including the 'Manchester Guardian' whose correspondent said:

> '...He played with much energy, certainty and brilliance, the 'Scotch Fantasie' of Max Bruch.
> Mr Eric Nicholson, one of the best English pupils trained by Dr. Brodsky, gave a refined and musicianly performance of the first movement of Beethoven's violin concerto. Mr Nicholson should become a well-known player'.

At home Eric developed his other main interests in art and literature and was known for the considerable amount of research he did into works by local artists of the eighteenth century and his collection of English watercolours. He also acquired a car registered as EC1, probably Westmorland's first independent registration. It is said that, when any local boys showed an interest, Eric was always delighted to show them his car, kept in a garage he owned at the house despite the fact that his mother rented the property from Martin Hodgson.

He took a great interest in Abbot Hall with which his family had some connection but his pleasure in the hall turned to despair as it slowly deteriorated at the hands of a series of owners. When he learned from Alderman Dobie that the Corporation was determined to demolish the Hall, Eric confided in him his hope that it should become an Art Gallery but admitted that he needed help to realise the vision because 'his own nervousness made him a very inadequate advocate'. Mr Francis Scott, brother of Sir Samuel who ran Provincial Insurance, financed a working party to look into the matter and, when it reported favourably, made a substantial contribution to the project managed by a specially created Trust. A public appeal was then launched to which local people responded generously, raising an amount which the Trust topped up to enable work to start. The gallery was opened by Princess Margaret in 1962.

Eric Nicholson found difficulty in making ends meet and at some stage in his life sold several treasures. His collection of watercolours and ceramics was sold to Peter Scott, who agreed to bequeath them on Eric's death to Abbot Hall. The house he inherited from his mother was bought by Lord Chorley. Known to Eric as Theodore, Chorley was a friend from school days and often visited Eric, parking his Rolls Royce outside the house. Chorley bought it on the understanding that Nicholson would live there until his death. In attempting to sell his violin in 1977, Eric encoun-

tered difficulties in proving its authenticity as an instrument made by Giovani Grancino about 200 years earlier. Eventually it was authenticated and sold in London.

When Nicholson died aged 88 on 14th November 1979 Abbot Hall benefited from the bequest, via Peter Scott, of his collection of watercolours and ceramics. These were first exhibited in the gallery in Spring 1980. A drawing of him by Bardy Crewdson also graced the foyer at that time.[22]

Bardy Crewdson's portrait of Eric Nicholson

Abbot Hall in its heyday long before its dilapidated state caused Eric Nicholson so much distress

TEMPORARY RESIDENTS

Various groups and individuals have lived on the Green who could be classified as 'temporary residents' because they chose to come to live on the Green for a limited period for specific purposes, were invited to visit residents of the Green, fled from elsewhere or were sent to the Green, or even banished there because of some real or imagined offence.

Lodgers and Boarders

Temporary residents in the shape of 'lodger' or 'boarder' appear in all of the four Censuses summarised in appendix 2. In each of the first three Ann Bradley of 5 Albert Road East (60 KG) had one lodger. These were the only ones listed in 1871 and 1881, but in 1891 four other houses were taking in lodgers including Ann's neighbour, Eliza Farrer at No. 6. The others were at 5 *Wood Lea* (5 KG) and 9 *Beechwood* (15 KG).

In 1901, the final year for which Census records are available, there were also five lodgers living on the Green, including one at each of the three houses, 4–6 Albert Road East. By this time, No. 5 was owned by a widow, Annie Fleming, who had inherited the house from her mother, Ann Bradley the previous year. Next door, Eliza Farrer's lodger was a John Lancaster, listed as an 'apprentice wood carver'. Perhaps he worked for

John Farrer, Eliza's son, a cabinet maker who lived at home? Then at No. 4, George Rigg – now retired – had a sub-inspector of schools lodging in his house. The other two lodgers in that year were a Church of England clergyman, Herbert Kelsey, living at 4 *Wood Lea* (4 KG) with Sarah Robson, while Elizabeth Williams, was boarding with the Dixons at *1 Fairbank* (17 KG).

All but one of the twelve lodgers recorded in the four Census years were born in England, most of them quite local to the Kendal area. The exception was Emma Thompson lodging with Ann Bradley in 1891 who, though a British citizen, was born in Cape Town.

It may be that lodgers and boarders lived on the Green beyond 1901. Certainly 5 Albert Road East was listed in a local directory of 1930 as still taking lodgers but no other evidence is available.

Refugees

No sooner had Holly Croft School closed than the house and the neighbouring pair – *Silver Howe and Overdale* – became home to a much larger and even more exotic group of temporary residents: Belgian refugees fleeing from the war in Europe. Over 70 of them came initially to Kendal as part of what we might now call a 'dispersal policy', and were accommodated in the four houses on the Green and at *Prospect* in Queen's Road. Since the end of July 1914 150,000 refugees had fled from Belgium and those parts of France also overrun by the German army. So cities and towns around the UK were exhorted by Herbert Samuel, the President of the Local Government Board, to share in taking care of them.[23]

The arrangements for looking after refugees in Kendal were made by a Committee of the Society of Friends; Arthur Simpson, the well-known local carver and furniture designer, was its secretary. He received considerable support from Mary Snowden Braithwaite who gave *Holly Croft* over to the reception of several families and rented for the same purpose another house – probably *Silver Howe* and *Overdale* (23–24 KG), next door, owned by Martin Hodgson.

Briefly some were accommodated in the Braithwaite's house, Ghyll Close, until other arrangements could be made. Mary also supplied clothes and other necessities for the refugees and was energetic in drawing in others to help.

The early refugees came in two groups, met with much pomp and ceremony by local dignitaries, witnessed by a great crowd of well-wishers at Oxenholme Station in October. The first group were taken to *Holly Croft* to meet several young women charged with caring for them. A reporter who witnessed their arrival described the newcomers patronisingly as peasants who 'are different in their domestic life from the same clans in this country. Their needs are few... meals are frugal but wholesome. The dish which finds tremendous favour with them is a sort of porridge made with lentils'.

A Belgian woman who lived before the war in London came to Kendal as matron. She acted as interpreter for the refugees of whom only one, a girl, spoke French, the remainder speaking a 'Dutch patois'. At Easter 1916 Gertrude Evans, a matron at Dalton House, the boys' boarding house for Stramongate School, came to care for the refugees.

Those refugees who moved into *Holly Croft* early on cleaned the neighbouring houses and helped prepare them for the next group from whom they hoped to get news of Belgium and, with luck, their own towns and villages. The women also knitted garments for British soldiers in khaki wool they had begged to be given once they understood that this is what many other local women were doing.

We are also told that their children were well provided with toys but seemed to enjoy most 'their day at the Catholic School, where they met the kindly disposed English children and those noble, great-hearted Sisters'. All the refugees were Catholics and found 'their greatest joy in Kendal... in the presence of Father Stevenson and the Sisters of the Convent'.

In time, harrowing stories of their escape were told by the refugees, many of whom had lost family and friends in German attacks on their towns and villages. One woman from Malines, who already had three children of her own, took charge of four teenagers who attached themselves to her during their flight. Eventually by travelling mostly by night and hiding in daylight they had managed to escape.

Some of the men among the refugees, who seemed to find it more difficult than the women to settle into their new homes, were employed around the town. A few of them made sabots in Arthur Simpson's workshop. Language difficulties made it hard to sort out the kind of timber they favoured but this problem was solved when the workshop foreman took them out into a woodland where they pointed out a beech tree as the usual source of raw material.

In accounts published after the last of the refugees had returned home Arthur Simpson noted that, altogether, 133 had been dealt with by the Committee for Kendal and District. A total of £3,370-10s-6d had been raised and disbursed by the Committee to cover their care, not including the value of various gifts and the free use of houses for accommodation. Their number had dwindled as arrangements were made for some

Simpson's cabinet workshop c. 1912.[24]

refugees to be cared for elsewhere or they had found work or moved to live nearer friends and relatives in other areas. In the final year only 54 had remained in Kendal; the last group left on 27th March 1919, seen off at the station by the mayor and a party of other worthies of the town.[25]

Unmarried Mothers

At around this time, other temporarily homeless people came to live at *Holly Croft*. Its name was changed to *St. Monica's*, listed in a business directory as a 'maternity home. But it was not just any such home, but one set up specifically for the care of unmarried mothers and their babies. The house was supervised by a committee of local people which included Mary Snowden Braithwaite, a sign of her usual willingness to work with people from other churches despite her own strong commitment to the Society of Friends. In 1929 Edith Peach was installed as matron but five years later, still under the same name, the home was relocated to Sedbergh Road.

From the baptism records of St Thomas' church it seems that 141 children were born at *St. Monica's* on Kendal Green between 1917 (which suggests they overlapped with the Belgian refugees) and 1934. Of this total born during the whole 18 year period, 102 were baptised in the last seven years; so perhaps it is not surprising that the larger house in Sedbergh Road was needed.

Servicemen and Prisoners of War

Only five years later *Holly Croft*, by then divided into two houses as originally intended, received other temporary but intermittent and exotic visitors from a very different background; men who had willingly left not only their homes but their homelands in order to fight in the Second World War. They were guests of two families – Arthur Duckworth, his wife Helen and daughter Barbara together with Arthur's brother Percy with his wife, Peggy and son David – who moved in 1939 from a house in Windermere Road to *1 Holly Croft (25 KG)*.

At about the time of the Battle of Britain various servicemen arrived in the UK to fight in Europe. Among them were airmen from Australia, Canada and New Zealand some of whom were entertained, between 1943 and 1945, by the Duckworth families as part of a scheme designed to give hospitality to servicemen during their leave periods. One reason is said to

The two airmen in this photograph are Canadians, George the pilot (on the left) and one of his crew-members (name unknown) separated by Helen Duckworth. Percy and Peggy Duckworth, her brother-in-law and sister-in-law, are to the right with their son David in the front.

The visitors here are two Australian pilots: Monty sitting on the wall between David and his father while Wal sits on the ground. Peggy is in the chair. On the wall next to David is a wind-up gramophone with the speaker door open.

have been to keep them away from 'flesh-pots' – unless one considers this applies to dances held in Kendal Town Hall!

The Duckworths' guests were being trained at bases around England as aircrew to carry out very hazardous bombing missions over Europe including, latterly Germany. Those that 'passed out' at the end of an arduous period of training lasting several months began a series of tours of duty each involving 30 night raids before the next period of leave. Many were lost in action during the first tour of duty, presumed dead, shot down over enemy-held territory. Those who did survive often found the prospect of further missions very difficult to deal with. Even after the war in Europe had finished those who still visited the Duckworths continued to be involved in flights over the Continent on so-called 'Spam' missions, dropping food supplies or propaganda leaflets.

For the brief periods their exotic guests spent at *Holly Croft* the Duckworths did their best to provide a period of rest when they could relax and escape the intense emotional and physical demands of the lives they usually led. After the last of them had left for home on six week voyages to Australia, life at *Holly Croft* seemed very quiet and uneventful.[26]

In what might be seen as a symmetrical act of kindness, German and Italian prisoners of war were entertained very briefly on Kendal Green. A group of them worked at the Sandes Avenue brush factory of Rainforth Hodgson of which Alfred Crossley was the owner-manager. His son George collected the POWs each day from the Bela Camp at Milnthorpe where they were billeted, took them to a wood near the 'Drunken Duck', north of Hawkshead, to crop timber for use in the brush factory, and returned them to the camp in the evening. George did not find it easy to relate to the German prisoners but befriended a number of the Italians for whom he felt sorry, particularly the younger ones, sometimes not much more than 18 years old. On Christmas Day, 1945, the year George and his family came to live at 4 *Beechwood*, they entertained a number of the Italians there. Meanwhile, several of the Germans were guests of his father, only five doors away, at 5 *Wood Lea*.

But the story did not stop there. George, who had learned Italian with the POWs' help, corresponded with some of them after the war. Years after his death, George's widow, Jane, and son, Michael, followed up the correspondence to make contact again with one of the ex-prisoners, Gigi, who managed the Continental Hotel in Loano on the Italian Riviera. In the late 1960s they visited him in Italy staying at his family home in Cunéo and then travelled to Loano to spend a week at his hotel.[27]

Residents of Care Homes

Finally, there are those who come to be cared for in houses on the Green. An early example is the purchase in 1974 of *Oakdene* by the Garthwaite Community, established two years earlier in Kendal to provide homes for handicapped people. Under the chairmanship of James Cropper the Trust raised sufficient funds to buy the house in 1974 and modify it to accommodate four staff and a group of mentally handicapped children. By the end of 1974 eleven children lived there, aged from two to sixteen years, sponsored by local authorities from around Britain. They were cared for by house parents Eric Hoyland, a social worker, and his wife Anne, a state registered nurse.[28] A management committee under the chairmanship of Mr Brian Hewertson had overall responsibility for the home; Mrs Eileen Russell of *Empson Hill* was the committee's secretary. The trust continued to run *Garthwaite* independently until 1979 when it became a Cheshire Home.

In January 1987 the home was closed down when only four children remained in residence and there was little chance of further admissions. Reasons for the decline in numbers are not clear although it is known that more handicapped children were being cared for in their local communities.[29]

At some later date, the name reverted to *Oakdene* when it became a residential home for older people which it is to this day.

Highfield was used for the same purpose when it was bought by a Mrs Stanley in 1979 who set up 'Westmorland House Residential Home' there. The present owners acquired it from her in December 1984 and continued to run it as a residential home until 1997. At some date a large extension had been built onto the back of the house.

Other elderly people lived at 25 Kendal Green – previously 1 *Holly Croft* – until it closed down in 1997. In the same year, however, it was reopened by the New Era Housing Association as a residential home for younger people cared for by NHS staff.

CHAPTER VII

KENDAL GREEN TODAY

WHAT IMPRESSION OF Kendal Green might someone have who returned after many years absence? As for the houses, those who were here recently enough to have seen the last of those built on the Green would probably not notice much difference in them. Even someone of a hundred years of age would recognise without difficulty the houses that existed early in the 20th century around the main part of the Green. Looking at the old photographs included in chapter three, it seems that little has changed except the occasional modification of bay windows, for example, or the insertion of the ubiquitous Velux roof-light. Since the designation of the Green as a conservation area in 1997 any further noticeable change in the appearance of the houses is unlikely.

In the spirit of conservation the Victorian greenhouses built for Joseph Jordan in the garden of *Oakdene* were renovated by Will Williams in the late 1990s. They were part and parcel of that piece of *Oakdene's* garden on which, in 1937, *The Newlands* was built, where Will and Sheila Williams live.

The built environment is unlikely to change much now that development in the immediate vicinity has stopped for lack of vacant sites. The only scope for in-filling locally is on a small roadside field at Helsfell Hall farm, Windermere Road, just before the town's limits and the large plot of land between Burneside Road, near Kentrigg, and the Kendal to Windermere Railway. Those who live in the estate being built there will probably be delighted that the re-laying of the rail track in 2002 has reduced considerably the clatter of passing trains.

As it is, the existing housing stock is home to so many children of primary school age that, given its popularity, St Thomas' school is not able to cope with the demand. So some children who live on the Green travel to schools around Kendal.

As regards the Green itself and its immediate surrounding, if someone were able to return who knew them in the very early days, two things would probably strike them. On the positive side would be the trees; in midsummer they grace the Green with their varied beauty, responding to every shift in light and breeze and the slow progression of the sun. A less welcome and more surprising sight might be the parked cars that so detract from the 'Greenscape'. If the returnees arrived just before 9 am or after 3 PM they might also be astonished at the number of cars in which parents, usually mothers, bring their children to St Thomas' school and collect them at the end of the day.

On the grassy areas of the Green throughout the day they would see familiar activities, even though the dress of those taking part might occasionally shock, especially in very hot weather when local families picnic after school and at weekends. The extent to which those who exercise their dogs take the trouble to 'scoop the poop' might also surprise. On the other hand, most of the games played by youngsters would be familiar. Kites are flown occasionally and all sorts of ball-games go on, predominantly soccer, all year-round, joined by cricket in the summer and infrequent bursts of rounders, volley ball, tennis and badminton. Only the infrequent appearance of model aeroplanes, gliders and frisbees might be disconcerting.

Should returnees have arrived in the dark of a late summer evening in 2002, they may also have been as surprised – and perhaps as intrigued and delighted – as some of us locals were by an exhibition at the south end of the Green of juggling with 'fire sticks', flaring at each end like giant, two-ended matchsticks. A young man who lives in a flat in the old carpet mill is the star performer but he is often joined by a small band of 'apprentice' fire jugglers.

Over the last five years a significant change has taken place on the soccer scene: girls are taking a growing interest while far fewer of them are prepared to stand around in a giggling gaggle admiring 'the boys' as they indulge in flaunting their various talents. When the girls first began to take part in the games they were treated as passengers; even those who had the nous to run into a space rarely received the ball from one of their male team mates. But in 2002, it's already different; the most assertive of the girl players are getting stuck in and refusing to be fobbed off with a 'bit part'. Sometimes a small group will be out there on their own practising skills. From now on they'll probably be back each year with greater effect.

Serious games of soccer continue the tradition of Kendal Green as when, on at least one weekday evening during the summer, a group of young men come to play. They set out their tall road cones as goal posts and don sets of 'bibs' to distinguish the teams in preparation for a vigorous and often quite noisy game.

For those aware of much earlier episodes, there is a certain déja vu as residents complain about the footballers' behaviour. In response, the Council – rather than the Kendal Fell Trustees as in the 19th century – attempts to mediate between residents and players. In the spirit of our times, on the last occasion when this occurred a consultative document was sent round to every house facing onto the Green to get people's views about the complaint. All was smoothed over eventually.

The last bonfire was only a few years ago, by which time it was huge and widespread, used as a repository for all sorts of waste material brought from around Kendal. Some lorries were driven onto the grass to dump their burden. What with this and the damage done by the extensive fire itself it was decided to call a halt. Even now, however, as the notices at the south end of the Green confirm, it is possible to arrange bonfires provided this is done under the auspices of a residents' association.

In fulfilling the role which previously accrued to the Kendal Fell Trust the Council is very active. Apart from ad hoc consultation about soccer and other particular questions, councillors for the local area consult Kendal Green residents on a wide variety of issues. Of special interest is the upkeep of the trees; when it is proposed to remove a diseased tree council officers talk to residents nearby to explain why it is necessary. Similarly, there is consultation about the planting of replacements and the pruning of damaged trees especially where they overhang the road and risk damaging passing vehicles. Given the relatively low volume and speed of traffic around the Green in its early days this was not a major issue for the Kendal Fell Trust.

In 2002 the local councillors arranged a well-attended evening meeting at St. Thomas' School to consult more widely on issues that were of concern as well as some discussion of what people liked about the area. Smaller follow-up meetings were held, attended by police and local government officials, to make progress with such themes as traffic, parking, vandalism and the local environment more generally.

Problems of vandalism of one sort or another have probably been endemic during the life of the Green although, whereas now the finger is pointed at youths from Hallgarth, earlier the Fell Trustees tended to be dealing with those reputed to have come from the 'Blue Buildings' at the bottom of Caroline Street. The problem today is probably more acute given the looser rein on which many young people seem to be held by their families and their greater anonymity within larger, less tightly knit communities. One manifestation of this change is the formation of a 'Neighbourhood Watch' among those who live in the north-east extension of the Green mirroring, perhaps, the Kendal Green Protection Association of which Theodore DeRome was the spokesman in the late 1880s.

In recent years a different social group has been created, as an informal association of residents involving people from over half of the houses on Kendal Green and a few nearby. They meet every quarter or so, taking part in a Jacob's Join in each other's houses.

It is difficult to compare the make-up of Kendal Green households with, say, a hundred years ago because there is no modern Census data. Even so, some differences are very clear as in the growing trend over a long period for some couples to live together without getting married and for more women with families to go out to work. As regards jobs done, it is probable that a smaller proportion of residents of the Green are local tradesmen or businessmen. However, there are still many who work as managers in assorted organisations, private and public, as well as architects, surveyors and engineers. Just as in 1901, many people are employed in public service, as local government officers and, especially, teachers. Involvement in the arts continues in the work of a very successful weaver whose tapestries are exhibited around the world, in the recent graduation in Fine Arts of a young mother and in the activities of amateur painters, instrumentalists and singers.

Memories of some of the Green's earlier residents and events are invoked around the Green in the houses they designed – Nelson's *Holmfield* and Dyson's house nearby – and around town, in Blacow's mens outfitters in Elephant Yard and 'Brennands' in large gold letters down Finkle Street and the 'Black Hog' on the wall above the Halifax Building Society. In the Brewery Arts Centre, Arthur Miles stares out at us from that magnificent photograph of the Whitwell Marks employees in 1910 around which an exhibition is planned for 2003.

In 2002 the 'Mushroom' on Scout Scar, believed by some of his descendants to have been designed and built by Alfred Nelson, was reopened after refurbishment in time for Queen Elizabeth's Golden Jubilee on 3rd June. The shelter has a new, stainless steel, dome; inside its rim of the same material a 360 degree panorama has been etched, showing all the mountains and hills visible on a clear day. Among those who witnessed the ceremony was Marion Winchester, one of Nelson's granddaughters, who also provided information for this narrative.

Alfred Wainwright's memory is maintained continuously through the

The MUSHROOM four-way shelter
was built in 1912
to commemorate the Coronation of King George V.
It was refurbished in June 2002
by Underbarrow & Bradleyfield Parish Council
on the occasion of the Golden Jubilee of his Granddaughter
Queen Elizabeth II.

The refurbishment was made possible by generous support from
The National Lottery Awards for All,
Cumbria County Council, Windermere & Staveley Neighbourhood Forum.
The General Public & Local Trusts,
Societies & Associations.
The Kendal South Westmorland Rotarians
and others who gave voluntary help.

*For accuracy, stand behind the central vertical rod
and use it to align the feature on the ground
with the detail on the map.*

John Coopey at the 'Mushroom'. Inserted is the plaque commemorating the Queen's Golden Jubilee.

use of his books by many who walk on local fells, including people who live on the Green. One of his great admirers is Colin Rowley, a retired geologist who now owns the house built for Wainwright; Colin is steadily 'bagging' all of the walks Wainwright described and illustrated so well.

Finally, after this book is published, it may be possible – as Curwen suggested 102 years ago – to put up a plaque that invokes and commemorates not a person, but how, on 25th April 1864, the Shakespeare Oak was planted and this gem of a place was called 'Kendal Green'.

SOURCES

GENERAL

Deeds of some Kendal Green houses
Cumbria Records Office
Planning applications, WSMB/K series
Rate Books
Minutes of Kendal Fell Trust 1861–1907
Material deposited on Holly Croft School and Shaw's Architectural
  Practice
Kendal Library
Census records 1861–1901
Electoral registers
Kelly's directories
Various folders of information and photographs

CHAPTERS

Chapter I

1 Marshall, J.D., 'Kendal in the late seventeenth and eighteenth
   Centuries', *Transactions of the Cumberland and Westmorland
   Antiquarian and Archaeological Societies (TCWAAS)*, Vol. LXXV, 1975,
   pp. 188–257.
2 *Ibid.*

3   Cumbria Records Office (Kendal), WSMB/K Box 14

4   Watterson, A., 'Working-class Housing and Related Health Policies in Mid-Nineteenth Century Kendal with Particular Reference to the Activities of John Whitwell, MP, *TCWWA*, 1987, Vol. LXXXVII, 1987, pp. 183–214.

5   *Ibid.*

6   *Ibid.* p. 205.

7   'Bye-Laws passed and approved on the 15th Day of September, 1863, by the Kendal Fell Trustees… pursuant to the Kendal Fell Act 1861. Printed in Kendal by Thomas Atkinson, 1864'.

8   (a) Satchell, J. 1984. *Kendal on Tenterhooks*, Kendal Civic Society and Frank Peters. Kendal

    (b) Bingham. R. 1995. *Kendal: A Social History*. Cicerone Press, Milnthorpe.

9   Buchanan, R.A. 1974. *Industrial Archaeology in Britain*. Book Club Associates, London.

10 Homan, R. 'The Kendal Union Building Societies', *TCWWAS*, Vol. LXXXII, 1982, pp. 184–190.

11 *Ibid.*

12 Bryer, T.P. 'A History of Kendal Green Wesleyan British School' – Part 1: *Wesley Historical Society Cumbria Branch Journal*, No. 36, Autumn 1995, pp. 2–11
    Part 2: No. 37, Spring 1996, pp. 16–22.

13 Curwen, J.F. 1900. *Kirkbie Kendal*. J. Wilson, Kendal.

Chapter II

1   From the deeds of 16 Green Road and 6 Wood Lea

2   Wainwright, A. 1997. *Kendal in the Nineteenth Century*. Westmorland Gazette, Kendal.

3   Lowe, N. 1998. *Mastering Modern British History (3rd ed.)*. Macmillan, London.

4   Bulmer, T.F. (Ed.) 1885. *History, Topography and Directory of Westmorland etc.* Bulmer & Co., Manchester.

5   The relationship between Charles Fildes and *Overdale* was drawn to our attention by John Satchell who referred us to his book: Satchell, J. 1996. *Family Album: Edwardian Life in the Lake Counties*. Sutton Pubishing Limited, Stroud.

6   The information about *Empson Hill* was provided by Eileen Russell and Michael Bottomley.

Chapter III

1 Bryer, *Op. Cit.*
2 From a 'Circular issued 20 April 1872' by a committee set up to manage the building of Kendal Green British School.
3 Bryer, *Op. Cit.*
4 Chart of Kendal's twentieth century Architecture 1900–1940 published by Kendal Civic Society.
5 Bryer, *Op. Cit.*
6 *Westmorland Gazette*, 31 October 1986.

Chapter IV

1 Curwen, *Op. Cit.*
2 *Handbook: Serpentine Nature Trail*, Wildlife Trust, Cumbria and SLDC.
3 *Westmorland Gazette*, 23 February 2001.
4 Peter Fox recorded this story.
5 Westmorland County Football Association (WCFA), 1997. *100 Years of Association Football in the County of Westmorland*. WCFA, Kendal.
6 Confirmed in a letter of 20 August 1971, retained with the deeds of 60 Kendal Green, from the Town Clerk to Thomas H Kevill & Co., Solicitors, in response to a query during a change of ownership.
7 Satchell (1996), *Op Cit.*, pp. 102–103.
8 Duff, M. and P., 1992. *Kendal in Old Photographs*. Sutton Publishing, Trowbridge.
9 *The Kendal Fell Act*, 1861, XXIX, p. 14.
10 Thistlethwaite, J., 1995. *Cumbrian Women Remember*. Thyme Press, Kendal.

Chapter V

1 These notes on the background of Quaker Trustees were derived from Donald Rooksby's, *The Man in Leather Britches*, published by him in 1994, and his *Quaker Guide to Kendal*.
2 Somervell, J. 1924. *Isaac and Rachel Wilson, Quakers of Kendal 1714–1785*. The Swarthmore Press Ltd., London.
3 Satchell (1984). *Op. Cit.*, Bingham, *Op. Cit.*, and a personal communication from Miss Tessa Wilson.
4 Atack, J., 'The History of the house of Samuel Gawith', *Tobacco*, 1 August, 1935.
5 This information about William Dixon's stock house designs was provided by his son Harry Dixon.

6 Satchell (1996), *Op. Cit.*
7 *Ibid.*
8 Cumbria Records Office (Kendal) WSMB/K/K45

Chapter VI

1 This information is taken, almost verbatim, from correspondence
   with Mike and Joan Mellor of Linlithgow. It arose from their
   researches into Joan's ancestors which gives them to understand that
   she may be related to John Birkett.
2 From an appreciation of Isaac Braithwaite by W.E. Wilson in *The
   Friend*, lxix, 1st March, 1929
3 From an appreciation of Mary Snowden Braithwaite by W.E. Wilson,
   The Friend, lxxi, 23 January 1931
4 Memorial Notice, Ackworth Old Scholars Association, *Report*, xciv, 1975
5 From correspondence with Nancy Walker (née Gawith) and an obituary in the *Old Stramonian, 1966/7*
6 From 'A Memoriam' on the death of John Whitwell, Esq., MP,
   November 1880, *Kendal Mercury*
7 *Westmorland Gazette*, 11 March 1922
8 This account is based on *A History of Goodacre Carpets*, (Joanna
   Wilson, 1989, from the company's archives) and recollections of Pat
   Dixon, David Dodds' granddaughter, based on newspaper cuttings an
   d photographs in her possession.
9 Curwen, *Op. Cit.*
10 Bingham, *Op. Cit.*, p. 326.
11 These notes are based on a diary of Ronald and Alice Pickles' life at
   Pinewoods, prepared by their daughter Janet, borrowed from Norman
   and Ann Ellis who bought the house from the Pickles.
12 This information was provided by Angela Day who earlier in her
   career as a pharmacist worked for F. W. Boon and Son.
13 Obituary, *The Westmorland Gazette*, 18 February 1911.
14 Bryer, T.P. 'William Gardiner (1860–1940): Head Master of Kendal
   Green School for 41 Years'. *Wesley Historical Society Cumbria Branch
   Journal*, No. 38, Autumn 1996, pp. 15–18.
15 'Kathleen M. Wilson, BA: A Tribute'. *The Old Stramonian*, 1963, pp.
   10–12.
16 Bingham, *Op. Cit.* p. 411.
17 Bingham, *Op. Cit*, p. 341.
18 Obituary, *Westmorland Gazette*, 6 October 1928.

19 Pattinson, G. 1981. *The Great Age of Steam on Windermere.* The Windermere Nautical Trust, Windermere.

20 *Westmorland Gazette,* 9 September 1865, p. 5.

21 Satchell (1996), *Op. Cit.,* pp. 141–2.

22 Based on an appreciation of Eric Nicholson by M.E. Birkett, Director of the Abbot Hall Gallery and an obituary by 'JSN', both in the gallery's journal, *Quarto,* vol. XVIII, No. 1, April 1980; an obituary in the *Westmorland Gazette,* 23 November 1979; and firsthand information provided by Michael Crossley.

23 *The Westmorland Gazette,* 17 October 1914.

24 Davidson, E. 1978. *The Simpsons of Kendal: Craftsmen in Wood, 1985–1952. University of Lancaster.*

25 *The Westmorland Gazette,* 5 November 1919.

26 This account is based on an illustrated diary produced specially for us by Barbara Webb (née Duckworth) who lived at *1 Holly Croft* from 1939 to 1950.

27 Information provided by Marjorie Crossley, daughter of the late Alf Crossley.

28 *Lancashire Evening Post,* 17 April 1975.

29 *Westmorland Gazette,* 5 December 1986.

APPENDIX I

SUMMARY OF INFORMATION ON
KENDAL GREEN HOUSES IN NUMBER ORDER

a) Nos. 1–30 – all built on Kendal Fell land except 1-6, on Wakefield's land

No./name	Date	Developer	Architect/builder	Comments
1-6: Wood Lea	1885	Hodgson & Levens	Levens/Levens	Detail in text
7-16: Beechwood	1886	Ditto	Ditto	Ditto
17-18: 1&2 Fairbank	1882	Wiper, Hodgson & Levens	Assume Levens	Ditto
19-20: Laurel Mount & Holly Bank	1883	Ditto	Ditto	Ditto
21: Oakdene	1884	Jordan (owner)	S Shaw/not known	Ditto
22: The Newlands	1937	Dodds (owner)	Not known	Ditto
23-24: Silver Howe & Overdale	1902	Hodgson	Hodgson jun./ not known	Ditto
25-26: 1&2 Holly Croft	1905	Hodgson	Ditto	Ditto
27: Pinewoods	1937	Pickles (owner)	M Shaw/not known	Ditto
28-30: 1-3 Fairfield	1870/1	Robinson	Not known	Ditto

b) Nos. 36 - 49: built on land accumulated by Alfred Nelson, some sold by executors or later owners

No./name	Date	Developer	Architect/builder	Comments
36	> 1973			
37	1950	Miss Golightly	Not known	Land sold by Gawith
38	1949	Alfred Wainwright	Ditto	Ditto
39	1936	John Alsop	Ditto	Ditto
40	1935	Mrs Thorpe	Ditto	Ditto
41: Holmfield	1905	W.A. Nelson (owner)	Assume Nelson	Detail in text
Holme Parrock	1985	R J Burrow	Self-build	Land sold by Dargue
42 & 43 (semi-det)	1931	Gawith/Dixon	W M Dixon	Land sold by Gawith?
44	1936	J Dyson (owner)	Dyson/not known	Detail in text
45: Hale Cote	1929	W Floyd (owner)	Not known	
46: Lynton	1925	E Brockbank	Ditto	
47: The Whins	1932	F Hoggarth (owner)	W Henry & G Dixon	Land sold by Gawith to builders
48 & 49 (semi-det)	1930	W Henry & G Dixon	Ditto	Ditto

c) Nos. 49a to 52 Kendal Green: all built on Kendal Fell lands, purchased directly from the Trust early on or, in the case of 49a & b, from the Town Council

No./name	Date	Developer	Architect/builder	Comments
49a	1955	J & E Johnson	Self-build	Completed 1957
49b	1964	D Russell (builder)	Not known/Russell	Bought in 1965 by Mr & Mrs Sutcliffe
50: Highfield	1880	G Lyon (owner)	Not known	More detail in text
51 & 52: Fernlea	1882 ?	W Simpson	Not known	Ditto

d) Four bungalows built on land owned by Lord Wakefield

No./name	Date	Developer	Architect/builder	Comments
Empson Hill	1964	D Russell	Bottomley/Russell's co.	More detail in text
Hillside	1956	Mr Bavin (owner)	Not known	
Thorncroft	1959	N Proctor	Ditto	
Zenith	1959	Ditto	Ditto	

e) Nos. 53 to 65, all built on Kendal Fell land offered for sale in 1862

No./name	Date	Developer	Architect/builder	Comments
53: Denmark House	1867	R Butterwith (owner)	G Rigg	More detail in text
54 & 55: semi-det.	1865	Burrows (54) & Gaskell (55)	Ditto	Similar design to 63-65
56-59: terrace	1922	W Dixon	W Dixon	More detail in text
60 & 61: semi det.	1866	Rigg & Burnett	G Rigg	Ditto
62: completes terrace	1935	A Langhorne (owner)	Not known	
63-65: terrace	1864	John Birkett	G Rigg	Ditto

APPENDIX II

CENSUS SUMMARIES, KENDAL GREEN:
1871, 1881, 1891 AND 1901

1871 Census

House name/no.	Occupiers	Occupation: head of household	Children*	Other residents
1 Fairfield	Miss. R Whitwell	Living on interest		2 sisters, 1 brother, 2 servants
2 Fairfield	Uninhabited			
3 Fairfield	Uninhabited			
1 Albert Road East	Mr & Mrs J Gibson	Chelsea pensioner	1D	
2 Albert Road East	Mr & Mrs J Banks	Surveyor & Land Agent		
3 Albert Road East	Mr & Mrs G Hall	Commercial Traveller	2 S	Mother-in-law, brother-in-law, servant
4 Albert Road East	Mr & Mrs G Rigg	Architect	1 S, 2 D	Visitor (Wesleyan minister)
5 Albert Road East	Mrs A Bradley	Retired innkeeper	1 D	Boarder, 2 visitors
6 Albert Road East	Mr & Mrs G Gaskell	Coal Dealer	1 D	Grandson
7 Albert Road East	Mr & Mrs J Dixon	Farmer of 60 acres		Servant
8 Albert Road East	Mr & Mrs R Butterwith	Grocer	2 S, 4 D	Aunt, servant

* S = son, D = daughter

1881 Census

House name/no.	Occupiers	Occupation: head of household	Children	Other residents
1 Fairfield				2 servants
2 Fairfield	Miss H Benson	Income from houses & land		Servant
3 Fairfield	Mr & Mrs H Martindale	County Treasurer	2 D	
1 Albert Road East	Mr & Mrs W Ion	Drapers' Manager	2 S, 1 D	Servant
2 Albert Road East	Temporarily absent			
3 Albert Road East	Mr F Nicholson	Commercial clerk		2 sisters, servant
4 Albert Road East	Mr G Rigg	Architect	2 D	
5 Albert Road East	Mrs A Bradley	Retired innkeeper	1 D	Son-in-Law, grandson, lodger and daughter
6 Albert Road East	Mrs E Farrer	Widow, annuitant	1 S	Servant
7 Albert Road East	Miss H Dixon	Ret'd farmers daughter		Father, mother, sister
8 Albert Road East	Mr & Mrs J Dodds	Ret'd civil engineer	1 D	Servant
Plus 3 houses being built…				

1891 Census

House name/no.	Occupiers	Occupation: head of household	Children	Other residents
1 Fairfield	Edward Whitwell	Widower, own means	3 D	2 servants
2 Fairfield	Mr & Mrs G Murdoch	Journalist		Servant
3 Fairfield	Agnes Martindale	Spinster, own means		Sister
Oakdene	Mr & Mrs J Jordan	Corn merchant	1 S, 1 D	Brother, niece, servant
Holly Bank	Mr & Mrs J Singleton	Civil Servant: Asst. to HM Inspector of Schools	2 S	Servant
Laurel Mount	Mr & Mrs A Grayson	Registered dentist	2 S, 1 D	Servant, nurse
2 Fairbank	Mr & Mrs D Pennington	General Manager, Iron Foundry	2 S, 4 D	Nephew
1 Fairbank	Mr & Mrs R Dixon	Bacon curer	2 S, 2D	Boarder
10 Beechwood Terrace	Mr & Mrs V Smith	Carpet designer	3 S, 2 D	
9 Beechwood Terrace	Mr & Mrs B Jopson	Grocer's assistant	2 S, 1D	Boarder, visitor
8 Beechwood Terrace	Mr & Mrs G Heywood	Grocer's assistant	1 S, 1 D	
7 Beechwood Terrace	Mr & Mrs A Handley	Baker	2 D	Father & mother-in-law, aunt, apprentice, 2 servants
6 Beechwood Terrace	Mr & Mrs J Wharton	Coal merchant	1 D	Sister-in-law, servant
5 Beechwood Terrace	Mr & Mrs F Nicholson	Secretary, Public Co.		Servant
4 Beechwood Terrace	Mr & Mrs T De Rome	Auctioneer, accountant, estate agent		Servant
3 Beechwood Terrace	Mr & Mrs J Illingworth	Tobacco & snuff manufacturer	1 D	Nephew, Servant
2 Beechwood Terrace	Mr & Mrs W Evershed	Brewery & analytical chemist	1 S, 1 D	Sister-in-law, 2 servants,
1 Beechwood Terrace	Uninhabited			

6 Wood Lea	Mr & Mrs J Ruthven	Commercial traveller	2 S	Servant
5 Wood Lea	Mr & Mrs J Graham	Banker's clerk	3 D	Boarder, servant
4 Wood Lea	Mr & Mrs W Gardiner	Schoolmaster	2 D	Servant
3 Wood Lea	Mr J Stubbs	Grocer's assistant (widower)	1 S, 1 D	Sister, housekeeper
2 Wood Lea	Mr & Mrs J Hewetson	Commercial traveller	1 S, 1 D	Visitor, servant
1 Wood Lea	Mr & Mrs T Thwaites	Living on own means		
1 Albert Road East	Mr T Hill	Retired schoolmaster (widower)	1 S, 1 D	
2 Albert Road East	Mrs E Higham	Widow (on own means)		Sister
3 Albert Road East	Mr & Mrs J Cloudsdale	Journalist	1 S, 1 D	Father-in-law, servant
4 Albert Road East	Mr G Rigg	Widower (own means)	2 D	
5 Albert Road East	Mrs A Bradley	Widow	1 D	Son-in-law, grandson, lodger, lady's maid
6 Albert Road East	Mrs E Farrer	Widow	1 S	Servant, lodger
7 Albert Road East	Mr & Mrs W Dinsdale	Boot and shoe maker	1 D	
8 Albert Road East	Mr C Butterwith	Grocer		Sister, nephew, great-nephew, niece, 2 servants
1 Fern Lea	Ms M Watson	Head of family, spinster		2 sisters
2 Fern Lea	Mrs C Illingworth	Widow	1 D	Servant
Highfield	Mr & Mrs G Lyon	House Painter	2 S	Servant

1901 Census

House name/no.	Occupiers	Occupation: head of household	Children	Other residents
1 Fairfield	Rachel Whitwell	Spinster		3 servants
2 Fairfield	Thomas Bradley	Retired, widower	1 S, 1 D	Grand-daughter, housemaid
3 Fairfield	Mr & Mrs W Harrison	Worsted spinner	3 S	Servant
Oakdene	Mr & Mrs J Jordan	Corn merchant	1 S, 1 D	Brother, niece, 2 servants
Holly Bank	Mr J Singleton	Sub-inspector of schools, widower	2 S	Sister-in-law, Servant
Laurel Mount	Mr & Mrs A Grayson	Dentist	2 S, 1 D	Servant
2 Fair Bank	Mr & Mrs D Pennington	Hydraulic Engineer	3 S, 2 D	
1 Fair Bank	Mr & Mrs R Dixon	Bacon curer	1 S, 1 D	Boarder
10 Beechwood Terrace	Mr & Mrs V Smith	Carpet designer and musician	2 S, 2 D	
9 Beechwood Terrace	Mr & Mrs B Jopson	Grocer's traveller	2 S, 1 D	
8 Beechwood Terrace	Mr & Mrs G Heywood	Grocer's assistant	1 S, 1 D	
7 Beechwood Terrace	Mr & Mrs D Anderson	Gardener & domestic	1 S, 3 D	Servant
6 Beechwood Terrace	Mrs M Tipper	Widow	3 S, 1 D	
5 Beechwood Terrace	Mr & Mrs F Nicholson	Secretary of Public Co.	1 S	Servant
4 Beechwood Terrace	Mr & Mrs T DeRome	Auctioneer & appraiser		Servant
3 Beechwood Terrace	Uoccupied			
2 Beechwood Terrace	Mr & Mrs J Ewen	Own means	2 S, 5 D	
1 Beechwood Terrace	Mr & Mrs S Rowling	Drysalter		
6 Wood Lea	Mr & Mrs J Ruthven	Commercial traveller	3 S, 1 D	Servant
5 Wood Lea	Mr & Mrs W Gardiner	Schoolmaster	1 S, 2 D	Servant
4 Wood Lea	Miss S Robson	Own means		Servant, lodger

3 Wood Lea	Mr & Mrs J Stubbs	Grocer's assistant	1 D	
2 Wood Lea	Mr & Mrs J Hewitson	Boot merchant	3 D	Servant
1 Wood Lea	Mr & Mrs J Parkinson	Retired farmer		Visitor
1 Albert Road East	Mr & Mrs J Gent	Tailor's cutter	5 D, 2 S	
2 Albert Road East	Mr & Mrs F Lewthwaite	Grocer shopkeeper		Mother-in-law, niece
3 Albert Road East	Mr & Mrs T Robinson	Farmer		
4 Albert Road East	Mr G Rigg	Ret'd architect, widower	2 D	Boarder
5 Albert Road East	Mrs A Fleming	Widow		Lodger
6 Albert Road East	Mrs E Farrer	Widow	1 S	Boarder
7 Albert Road East	Mr & Mrs W Dinsdale	Boot & shoe maker	1 D	
8 Albert Road East	Mr C Butterwith	Wholesale grocer		Sister-in-law, 2 nieces, 1 nephew, 1 servant
1 Fern Lea	Unoccupied			
2 Fern Lea	Mr & Mrs C Chorley	Retired licensed victualler	1 S, 1 D	Son-in-law, 2 grandsons, 3 grand-daughters, 1 niece
Highfield	Mr & Mrs G Lyon	House painter	2 S	Servant

Notes: Anderson's 3 daughters (7 Beechwood) all school mistresses.
Charles Tipper (son at 6 Beechwood) : 'Organising secretary, Technical education'
Lodger at 4 Wood Lea was C of E clergyman
Boarder at 4 Albert Road East was sub-inspector of schools
Boarder at 6 Albert Road East was apprentice woodcarver

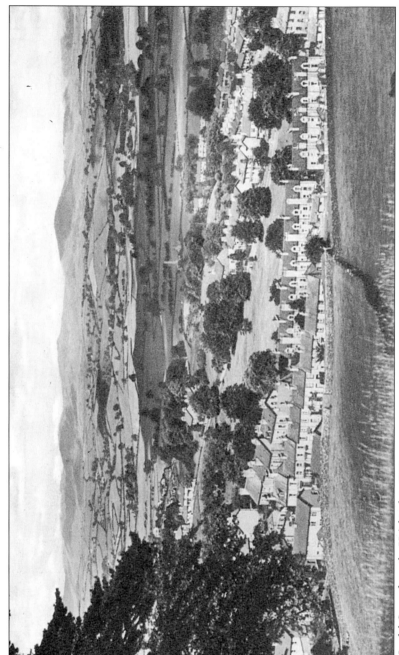

Kendal Green from the Heights, late 1920s

INDEX

IF YOU HAVE ENJOYED THIS BOOK YOU MAY ALSO ENJOY OTHER BOOKS
PUBLISHED BY HELM PRESS.

'A Westmorland Shepherd' His life, poems and songs

'Elephants On The Line' Tales of a Cumbrian Railwayman (1947-95)

'Dear Mr Salvin' The story of the building of a 19th century Ulverston
church

'All In A Lifetime' The story of a Dalesman as told to June Fisher

'Hawkshead Revisited" A Walk in time through Hawkshead

'A Century of Heversham and Leasgill' A walk in time through these
old Westmorland villages

'An Old Westmorland Garage' The story behind Crabtree's
of Kendal

'Ambleside Remembered' People and Places, Past and Present

'Snagging Turnips and Scaling Muck' The Women's Land Army
in Westmorland

'The Windermere Ferry' History, Boats, Ferrymen & Passengers

HELM PRESS
10 Abbey Gardens, Natland, Kendal, Cumbria LA9 7SP
Tel: 015395 61321
E-mail: HelmPress@natland.freeserve.co.uk